WILD COURAGE

Go After What You Want and Get It

—

JENNY WOOD

PORTFOLIO | PENGUIN

Portfolio / Penguin
An imprint of Penguin Random House LLC
1745 Broadway, New York, NY 10019
penguinrandomhouse.com

Most Portfolio books are available at a discount when purchased in quantity for sales
promotions or corporate use. Special editions, which include personalized covers, excerpts,
and corporate imprints, can be created when purchased in large quantities. For more
information, please call (212) 572-2232 or email specialmarkets@penguinrandomhouse.com.
Your local bookstore can also assist with discounted bulk purchases using the
Penguin Random House corporate Business-to-Business program. For assistance in
locating a participating retailer, email B2B@penguinrandomhouse.com.

LIBRARY OF CONGRESS CATALOGING-IN-PUBLICATION DATA
Names: Wood, Jenny (Executive coach), author.
Title: Wild courage: go after what you want and get it / Jenny Wood.
Description: [New York] : Portfolio/Penguin, [2025] | Includes bibliographical references. |
Identifiers: LCCN 2024054606 (print) | LCCN 2024054607 (ebook) |
ISBN 9780593717646 (hardcover) | ISBN 9798217045679 (international edition) |
ISBN 9780593717653 (ebook)
Subjects: LCSH: Self-realization. | Courage. | Success.
Classification: LCC BF637.S4 .W6585 2025 (print) | LCC BF637.S4 (ebook) |
DDC 158.1—dc23/eng/20241209
LC record available at https://lccn.loc.gov/2024054606
LC ebook record available at https://lccn.loc.gov/2024054607

Printed in the United States of America
1st Printing

The authorized representative in the EU for product safety and compliance is
Penguin Random House Ireland, Morrison Chambers, 32 Nassau Street,
Dublin D02 YH68, Ireland, https://eu-contact.penguin.ie.

TO MY SON, ARI, AND MY DAUGHTER, NOA:
MAY YOU HAVE THE COURAGE TO GO AFTER
WHAT YOU WANT—AND GET IT.

I believe it may be necessary to encounter many defeats without being defeated by them.

—MAYA ANGELOU

CONTENTS

CUT TO THE CHASE

———

If time is short and you're looking for quick, targeted help on key career and success topics, jump directly to hands-on advice as follows:

Shortcuts and summaries can be handy. That said, you'll receive the most benefit by reading this book from beginning to end. Either way, take courage—you're on your way to getting more of what you want.

WILD COURAGE

Gather Your Courage

I've gotta be me.

—SAMMY DAVIS JR.

Years ago, I chased a total stranger off the New York City subway. Today, he's my husband and the father of our two children. The wild courage I mustered that day has driven my professional achievements as well, first as a researcher at Harvard Business School, then as an executive at Google, where I climbed the ranks for nearly two decades, and now as an author, speaker, and consultant to Fortune 500 companies.

Why is courage essential to success? Because we are often timid on the inside. Every single one of us, including me. At Google, I conjured up plenty of fear: fear that I wouldn't impress my boss in our weekly one-on-one. Fear that I would say something stupid in that big meeting full of VIPs. Fear that no one would ever forget the presentation I flubbed. Cool and collected exec on the outside. *A lot* more going on on the inside. I realized that fear will always be my companion. But I have succeeded largely by pushing through that fear to achieve my heartfelt ambitions. That's where all ambitions hide: on the other side of fear.

This book will help you do the same: to feel the fear, acknowledge it, and set it aside. To unapologetically chase after what you want in life as though your life depends on it.

It does.

My experiences have taught me that to be successful, you must act as if you already are. In this book, I will help you find the courage to walk the path to success before you're successful. Here you will discover an arsenal of techniques to help you get ahead in your career, build stronger personal and professional relationships, promote your accomplishments with unshakable confidence, and more. The one thing that will help you stop worrying what others think and start moving toward your dreams is courage. Wild quantities of courage.

If you accept this book's challenge, you'll be astonished by what you discover. After a courageous act or two, you'll realize that many of your fears are just stories you're telling yourself. They aren't real. You can choose to listen to them . . . or rewrite them.

That said, fear isn't useless. It's actually a handy *compass*. When fear says, "Run away," it means you're chasing something important to you. Something *valuable*. Resist the urge to avoid the very behaviors that will accelerate your growth and maximize the chances of personal and professional success. To grasp the prize, you're going to have to reach, stretch, and get pretty *uncomfortable*. And that's scary! Fear is there to keep you safe . . . and small. When fear tells you to stop, you may have only a split second to decide. Don't balk. Think *wild courage* and go for it! Chase after what you want, whether it's the job of your dreams, the business you've always wanted to build, or, as was my experience on the subway, the ideal partner for you.

Wild courage will change your life.

When I turned thirty, I was riding the C train home from work when I noticed the gorgeous guy holding on to the car's middle pole twenty feet away from me. He was just my type: thick hair, five-o'clock shadow, beautiful eyes. Because he seemed artsy, I guessed he was a theatrical set designer, something along those New York lines. As the train rolled along the tracks, I came up with all sorts of stories about what he was doing and where he was going next.

There are no social norms around talking to people on the subway. You just *don't*. However, I decided that if the guy got off at my stop, Seventy-Second Street, I'd say hi, come what may. If not, I'd let it go.

He got off at Fifty-Ninth.

I thought, "Oh well, that's fate saying it wasn't meant to be." But then I remembered that I don't believe in fate! I make my own luck. Leaping to my feet, I darted through the crowd and squeezed through the subway doors as they closed.

As described in a *New York Times* article that went viral, I tapped the guy on the shoulder as he reached the station exit. Then, I took my huffing and disheveled shot at creating the life I wanted for myself: "You're wearing gloves, so I can't tell if you've got a wedding ring; however, if you're not married, you were on my subway, and I think you're cute. Can I give you my business card?"

Reader, Jon took the card.

"It was a pretty gutsy thing to do," Jon later told the *Times*. "That sort of thing appeals to me."

Too excited to wait for the next train, I walked the remaining thirteen blocks home, smiling, through a blizzard.

Serendipity isn't found; it's made.

Sure, my behavior was a little out there. The story of how I met my husband goes against *so many* unwritten rules. We're told all these stories about how we're "supposed" to meet a romantic partner, like the old notion that the man is supposed to pursue and the woman is supposed to play "hard to get." Or that when fate (i.e., luck) plays a role, it means the relationship was "meant to be." If I'd dutifully followed the arbitrary dating rules until things felt "meant to be" instead of summoning the courage to hustle off that train, I'd still be single.

I made my own "meant to be." All it took was wild courage.

This book is about getting what you want in life and why it's not talent, skill, money, or luck standing in your way—it's you.

You.

And that's such good news. It means that all you really need to do is overcome your limited mindset. Your self-defeating attitude. Your worries and fears. Once you quiet the stubborn inner voice telling you to hold back when you could be leaping forward, all the obstacles *out there* will no longer intimidate you.

You can let that voice stand in your way forever. Or you can take courage from a simple truth: *This is your life and no one else's.* Whatever you've been through and wherever you are right now, you can *always* take the wheel and drive. You have agency. All it takes is courage to push through your

- fear of the unknown,

- fear of discomfort,

- fear of failure, and

- most of all, *fear of the judgment of others.*

Brave these fears and nothing is beyond your grasp.

Ironically, we usually know what it will take to achieve our biggest ambitions, but we don't take action because we're worried about how it might look. We fear what other people, even strangers, will think of us if we carve a path instead of following the crowd.

The desire to fit in runs deep. Shake off these irrational fears, and you'll be free. Free to act on your behalf for the first time in your life.

Free to become your own champion. Everything you've ever wanted is on the other side of fear.

Again, this isn't about fear of heights or fear of clowns . . . unless you want to become a pilot or a circus ringmaster. When it comes to personal and professional goals, we're quaking with fear of the judgment of others. What friends, family, and even complete strangers will think about us if we seize the spotlight. This fear drives us to conform instead of conquer.

Successful people take action despite their fear. They muster the courage to do what's necessary to succeed before it's encouraged by others—or even considered socially acceptable. What they *don't* do is look elsewhere for permission or affirmation. They *don't* wait until everyone else is doing it. No, they just *act*. Others may judge them, but they persevere, confident that *success will justify their actions retroactively*.

Remember, we hear about innovators, entrepreneurs, artists, and others who inspire us only *after* their gambles have paid off. We rarely see how risky their actions looked before success transformed weirdness into authenticity and recklessness into courage. When someone achieves something extraordinary—developing a world-changing innovation, launching a successful business, directing a hit movie—we rub out all the daring lines they crossed to get there. In hindsight, the risks they took to reach the top look shrewd, wise, and perceptive. They didn't at the time.

Ironically, people will scour a successful person's bestselling memoir or viral social media post for advice. However, even with the road map for success in front of them, they will *still* hesitate to act because *they don't feel successful enough to pull it off*. Somehow, we never realize that **a success mindset** *precedes* **success.** That famous person didn't get away with doing what they did because they were famous. They became famous because they conjured the courage to try things they weren't guaranteed to pull off.

We see everything differently in the context of success. Where the intern's behavior is "weird," the boss's *identical* behavior is "authentic." Where the employee's decision to leave the company is "selfish," the owner's decision to sell the same company is "sensible." Where the business school grad's new solo venture is "reckless," the successful entrepreneur's start-up is "courageous." We're comfortable with risks only after we know they paid off. Unfortunately, time only moves in one direction. By the point a risk feels safe, the opportunity is long gone.

A mindset of wild courage will save you. Push past fear and the desperate need to please others, and you'll be free to follow good advice instead of wishing you were the kind of person who could. No one will ever give you that permission. You must give it to yourself. Don't let your fear of being labeled a certain way by others hold you back. Because these labels are ridiculous. We apply very specific ones to people who break social norms to get what they want: **WEIRD. SELFISH. SHAMELESS. OBSESSED. NOSY. MANIPULATIVE. BRUTAL. RECKLESS. BOSSY.**

These words don't paint a rosy picture. But think about it: What's actually wrong with being "weird"? In high school, being yourself (i.e., weird) gets you ostracized. But how long has high school been over for you now? Having been an executive for many years at one of the world's best companies to work for, I can tell you that standing out—being a little weird—gets you promoted. Be yourself or be forgotten.

Likewise, what's fundamentally wrong with being "selfish"? If you don't advocate for yourself, no one else will. Your manager has problems of their own. They don't necessarily wake up every morning wondering how to make *your* career flourish. Call it selfish if you want, but being your own champion is essential. As the legendary sage Rabbi Hillel wrote long ago, "If I am not for myself, who will be for me?"

Also, what's wrong with acting "shamelessly"? Why should anyone feel shame about going after what they want? I always wince when someone apologizes for the "shameless plug" of their own work. Plug away! Where does shame enter into it? Take pride in your accomplishments!

Was it shameless to offer a cute guy my business card? If my bold move had turned Jon off, he wouldn't have been right for me. What did I have to fear beyond some momentary embarrassment? Better to be my weird, selfish, and shameless self and start the relationship on an honest footing.

Negative labels like these are the bars of an invisible cage.

THE NINE TRAITS

In the following chapters, we will transform these nine labels into powerful Traits that will direct your efforts and fuel your courage. Through techniques and strategies validated by the many individual contributors, managers, and leaders I've taught and coached, I'll show you how each Trait functions as a powerful principle for success. Throughout the book, they will appear in bold when I refer to them in their refined, courageous sense versus their original, negative connotation:

- **WEIRD:** The courage to stand out.

- **SELFISH:** The courage to stand up for what you want.

- **SHAMELESS:** The courage to stand behind your efforts and abilities.

- **OBSESSED:** The courage to set your own standard.

- **NOSY:** The courage to dig deeper.

- **MANIPULATIVE:** The courage to influence others.

- **BRUTAL:** The courage to protect your time and energy.

- **RECKLESS:** The courage to take calculated risks.

- **BOSSY:** The courage to listen and lead.

Each **Trait** requires nothing more than courage. No special skill or talent is required. You can embrace them all from where you're standing, and they only get easier as you learn through experience that none are as uncomfortable and scary as they seem. Together, they will bolster you when that obnoxious inner voice speaks up:

- "I'm not going to say it that way! That would be weird of me."

- "We should do this differently, but I don't want to be bossy."

- "It seems like a good investment for someone else, but I wouldn't want to be reckless."

To be fair, these words carry negative connotations because some push them too far. Yes, some people really are selfish, manipulative, or reckless. But these are the exceptions that prove the rule. In my corporate experience, most employees overcorrect in the other direction. They let their fear of being seen as brutal prevent them from making hard but necessary choices. Or their fear of being seen as bossy from taking the lead when no one else will. And so on. It's for this majority that I've written this book—to level the playing field.

Because you can go too far with every **Trait**, each chapter will close with **Trait Traps**, simple guardrails to flag your attention when a strength threatens to become a weakness. **OBSESSED** is about adopting a vigorous work ethic, not spiraling into self-destructive work addiction and burnout. **NOSY** is about healthy curiosity, not invasive surveillance of coworkers. And so on.

When you find yourself balking at the next right action in your quest—from requesting a raise to starting a business to chasing after a stranger for their telephone number—do a little thought experiment. Ask yourself how you would feel if you already had power, success, and prestige. Is the action you're contemplating dangerous or unethical—or are you just worried that someone will think that *you* shouldn't do it?

I first helped people achieve this courageous mindset shift with Own Your Career (OYC), a career advice program I founded as a Google executive. Over the course of my eighteen years at Google, I'd ambitiously climbed my way up from an entry-level position to an executive role in a team that helped drive billions in revenue. Figuring I must have learned some useful lessons along the way, I started jotting down career insights, mostly as reminders to my future self. When some trusted peers saw the list and urged me to share it widely, I did, and I was as surprised as anyone when my advice became a company phenomenon, spreading throughout Google's offices worldwide and becoming one of the largest career programs in the company. OYC was an instant favorite among rookie "Nooglers" and veteran Google employees alike—we're talking 97 percent positive feedback from the tens of thousands of participants at the company.

My job involved leading an operations team sitting between sales and engineering; it had nothing to do with training and development. Yet I seemed to have stumbled onto a hidden strength. Why not run with it?

Operating the program as a passion project, I eventually realized that the stuff I wrote about applied to much more than advancing in a corporate career. Hidden between all the lines was the secret of how I'd gotten *all* the good things in my life: a loving family, great friendships, financial stability, and, yes, professional success. All the stuff I truly cherished. When things worked out, it was because I'd had the *courage* to do pretty much the opposite of what we're always told to do. To speak up when I was supposed to keep my head down. To disagree when it would be safer to go along with the crowd.

Contrary to how we're programmed growing up, success isn't about meeting someone's arbitrary standard of performance or behavior. Permission to reach for success never comes from outside. *You get what you want by having the courage to unapologetically chase after it.* Some people hear my subway story, or learn how I secured a particular professional opportunity, and label my behavior as aggressive. But is it "aggressive" to go after what you want *without* undermining yourself or disparaging your own efforts? That's not aggression. It's courage! The courage to pursue what you want.

A question I'm often asked is, "What should I do with my life?" What use is developing a success mindset if you don't know what success looks like for you? How do you courageously pursue a goal if you aren't sure what the goal is or where it ranks alongside all the other things you want in life?

Most of the time, existential doubt isn't about lack of ambition but overabundance of caution. While plenty of us don't know what we want, plenty more do. Those goals just feel out of reach, so we aim small rather than experience the discomfort of going after something we might not get. Setting a difficult goal can feel like asking for humiliation. If you admit what you want and fail to get it, other people might think you're a—*gulp*—human being. Not perfect. Just a person.

There we go again, limiting our vision rather than betting on ourselves.

To make progress, you have to set an ambitious course and accept the possibility of failure. If you enroll in a tough professional certification program, you might not make it through. Failure is a possibility. However, if you don't enroll, you *definitely* won't get that certificate. Failure is guaranteed when you don't try. So why not try?

It takes courage to commit yourself to achieving a single goal instead of half-heartedly pursuing several. Chase after many things for fear of failing to reach one difficult but important objective, and you won't go far in any direction. Yes, focus may not be enough to achieve your primary goal. But if you pursue your heart's desire with complete commitment and fail, the pain of loss also brings a lightness. Your heart is *free.* That thing you'd wanted so badly is off the table. It no longer occupies valuable space in your mind because you know you gave it your best shot. Now, you can turn your attention elsewhere.

Regret is much heavier than failure.

In my experience, most of our wild ambitions are more realistic than we think. When people talk to me about their lifelong goals, they act as though they're about to share an outrageous fantasy, only to point to something *eminently* achievable. We're so eager to discount ourselves that we dismiss the possibilities that are entirely within our reach. In most cases, all it will take is hard work, patience, and, above all, the courage to face the judgment of others.

When I'm ready to set a goal, I like to use a little formula I call **Rock, Chalk, Talk, and Walk**. This exercise will help you uncover and commit yourself to the path that matters most to you:

Rock. Identify the big achievement that would be most significant to you at this point in your life. This rock will be a heavy lift, but it will also give you the most dramatic return on investment of time and energy. Be honest with yourself: What would you choose if you could flip a switch and immediately reach one giant milestone? Don't hold back. Forget about "realistic." Make your goal measurable and specific, no matter how outlandish it feels. Not just "musician" but "professional touring musician with a Grammy-winning album."

Chalk. Write down what you want to do and give it a reasonable timeframe. Then work backward, laying out all the milestones along the way to moving your big rock. Again, plan for this goal like you would approach any work or personal project, from applying to graduate school to planning a house remodel.

Talk. Say your goal out loud: "By this time next year, I will X." Post your goal where you will see it daily. Tell the people in your life. If someone reacts to your idea poorly, don't let that sway you. Ambitious people cherish ambition in others, but the fearful feel threatened when others display the courage they lack. Remember, there's a difference between identifying potential roadblocks and saying you don't have what it takes.

Welcome constructive advice. Ally with people who respond to your stated goals with enthusiasm and support, not derision. (This is a great filter for relationships in general.)

Walk. The magic happens when you consistently take action toward your goal. That's all there is to it. Walk the talk. Without action, even the smallest ambition is a pipe dream.

Rock, chalk, talk, and walk. Goal setting in a nutshell.

WHY IT TAKES WILD COURAGE

You *must* stand out to get what you want. Standing out is your best—and possibly only—shot at success: A great career or thriving business. An amazing partner. Creative fulfillment. Public recognition. Whatever you're after, passive acceptance and anonymous invisibility won't help you catch it.

The reason we find it so hard to go out on a limb is because of our evolutionary roots. On the savanna, exclusion for *Homo sapiens* living in small tribes meant not only loneliness but certain death. Lions picked off the conspicuous. Early humans were as interdependent as any colony of ants or bees, and this heritage is baked deeply in our DNA. Acceptance by the tribe meant survival. That's why feelings like embarrassment, shame, and fear actually hurt. According to research by neuroscientist Jaak Panksepp and others, "certain human brain areas that 'light up' during physical pain are also activated during emotional pain induced by social exclusion." Pain is the body's way of protecting you. That is genuine pain you're experiencing when thinking about an embarrassing moment from high school.

We evolved in an environment where being ostracized meant becoming an appetizer. A loud warning bell goes off when we feel judged in front of others. Adrenaline flows, hands shake, voice quivers. To the most primitive parts of the brain, being evaluated by others threatens exile and even death. People tell pollsters they fear public speaking more than death itself. It's just a presentation, pal—you're in a lion-free zone. But the feelings are real.

On the savanna, our tribe was a small handful of people. In the modern world, the tribe is everybody, everywhere, all the time. Our close friends, our distant relatives, everyone in our professional industry, and anonymous trolls on social media. Breaking with convention to get what we want is difficult, painful, and scary because all eight billion human beings on planet Earth have the power to tell us we're not good enough and make it *hurt*. No wonder we play small, hoping no one notices us—even as we desperately wish they would.

Regardless of your emotions, **the world out there isn't your tribe**. These primal instincts lead people to believe that if they don't stand out or attract negative attention in any way, the tribe will provide for them. It once did. But no longer.

Working with and coaching leaders, entrepreneurs, scientists, and artists from all backgrounds, I've discovered a common element among high achievers: they never let the instinct to conform to this tribe's expectations steer them from their chosen path.

High performers are self-contained and self-directed. Instead of letting their friends, family, or academic peers set their bar for performance, they meet a self-determined standard and reject judgment. Whether surrounded by excellence or mediocrity, high performers establish their own definition of success and work steadily to achieve it.

At NYU, a group of students created a Facebook group: "Stefani Germanotta, you will never be famous." Stefani Germanotta isn't a household name, but Lady Gaga, her alter ego, is one of the world's biggest pop stars and actors. Germanotta succeeded not by ignoring the haters—impossible—but by pushing through the discomfort of negative feedback. Because the behavior of jealous peers in college wasn't relevant to her goal of becoming a famous performer, she shook it off—to paraphrase another similarly tenacious pop star.

Fighting conformity isn't easy to do. Teachers and parents incentivize us to fit in and win public favor from a young age. Before reaching adolescence, we're comfortable enforcing conformity among our peers—and in our own hearts. When we're thrust into the real world, however, the behaviors that would have gotten us labeled weird, selfish, shameless, and so on turn out to be the most richly rewarded.

Sometimes, the thing you want to chase after might involve stepping off the familiar path and forging into the unknown. If that's the case for you and you're nervous, I can relate. I haven't lived with wild courage every minute of my life. Not by a long shot. There have been many times when I let fear win. I've held back when I should have raised my hand, only to watch someone else run with an opportunity that should have been mine. I've performed below my ability—and gotten the performance scores to match. I've let other people steer me instead of carving my own path. In addition to the successes I share, you'll learn about my failures, hesitations, and missteps, too. This isn't about perfection. The **Traits** are simply guiding principles to help you keep chasing after what you want.

Leaving Google to help people achieve their goals full time as an author, speaker, corporate trainer, workshop facilitator, and coach scared me. But I knew that curiosity, like desire, can stifle fear. So I got **NOSY**. Instead of letting my imagination run wild with doomsday scenarios, I assembled evidence for and against my decision. By then, I'd received plenty of feedback on my efforts, and though I hate reading criticism as much as anyone, I read through everything—and discovered many positive signs of my impact. Feedback like:

- "You changed my life."

- "You helped me get my dream role."

- "This was the best career development training I've ever taken!"

Reading these messages fueled the **OBSESSED** part of me that was eager to help more people. I knew my passion extended beyond helping people advance within the walls of one, albeit enormous, tech company. I wanted to show many more people how to become happier, more confident, and more fulfilled in many other areas of life.

Even so, it was So Dang Hard to let go of the idea of being an executive at Google for the rest of my career. I struggled to wrap my head around a new reality, wondering what my colleagues would think about my decision to leave a successful career behind.

That's when my executive coach, Julie Connolly, paraphrased a simple but profound Buddhist saying:

Circumstances change.

That stopped me in my tracks.

Just because I'd always thought I'd be at Google for life didn't mean that my belief couldn't change, too. I had acquired so much knowledge in my journey, and I couldn't help wanting to share it with as many people as possible. Writing a book, this book, felt like the best way to do that. I just had to take my own advice and do what was right for me, no matter what others might think.

My circumstances changed. I changed. So I leaped, and landed here.

What about you? Have your circumstances changed? Are you chasing today's dream, or yesterday's? Your dream, or someone else's? Or are you simply stuck, waiting for permission to chase after what you want?

It's time to permit yourself. No one else ever will.

The book's website offers templates, scripts, and other tactical resources to complement your work with each of the Traits. For starters, head to wildcouragebook.com/resources and check out the **Welcome Kit**. It includes a short video training on how to put this book into practice, along with three crucial first steps.

1

WEIRD

Win as you or lose as "who?"

> **Weird**
>
> **(adj.):** of strange or extraordinary character.
>
> **Weird redefined:** The courage to stand out.

Before catching the right man on the New York City subway, I embarked on a painful, long-drawn-out chase after the wrong one: "Brian." Instead of moving on when the wrongness of the match became obvious—to any rational person, anyway—I refused to accept defeat. By the time I stopped twisting my authentic weirdness into his idea of normal, I'd done real damage to myself.

Never again.

There is no normal. We're all **WEIRD** in different ways. I'm bold, outspoken, driven, confident, and a bit loud. I dance down the sidewalk in public while listening to a cappella Broadway show tunes on my headphones. I've never been one to play it cool, dim my light, or curb my enthusiasm, and some people find me odd or a "bit much."

My attributes have always been strengths or weaknesses, depending on the context and how well I've leveraged them. Unfortunately, with

Brian, my iron determination quickly became a weakness. From the start, he wanted someone demure and quiet. A wallflower. More accurately, a blond and petite wallflower. Ignoring this disconnect, I pursued him, and eventually, we started dating. Sort of.

"I want to be with someone gorgeous but insecure," Brian once told me. "Someone who doesn't realize how pretty she is." How do you respond when someone you're supposedly dating says that? However, as embarrassing as it is to admit, Brian's distancing behavior drove me to continue chasing him. The more he pulled back, the more I leaned in, becoming less myself while getting no closer to becoming the person he really wanted.

Short of dyeing my hair blond, I did everything I reasonably could to fit Brian's specifications: I behaved demurely, spoke quietly, and even *dressed* differently. When Brian suggested I wear tighter jeans, my heart sank. But I bought the jeans anyway.

It took six full years of flirtation, dating, friends with benefits, and "what even *is* this?" conversations to hit bottom. While I was squatting in the rubble of my old self, it finally struck me: I would *never* be Brian's person. Mustering the courage, I made a clean break. (See **BRUTAL** for more on those.) One of the best decisions I've made, however late. If you keep squeezing your square peg into a round hole, you'll get bent out of shape.

Brian has wonderful qualities. To this day, I think of him fondly. My **WEIRD** just wasn't compatible with his. In retrospect, my reluctance to abandon pursuit drove some of his questionable behavior. I needed someone who wanted me as I was. Learning to own my **WEIRD** instead of repressing it rescued me from endless heartbreak and set me on the path toward finding the love of my life. Embracing my authentic self also elevated my other personal and professional relationships, improving my life and accelerating my career.

Are you ready to own your **WEIRD**?

IN DEFENSE OF BEING A LITTLE WEIRD

After World War II ended, US fighter pilot casualties kept rising. The air force suspected the cockpit design. Pilots were struggling to reach the controls while maneuvering, with disastrous consequences. What was happening? Why didn't cockpits fit their pilots anymore?

Had the average pilot gotten larger since the 1920s? After all, the American diet had become more abundant. To his surprise, Gilbert S. Daniels, the Harvard-educated lieutenant assigned to solving the problem, discovered that the "average pilot" didn't exist in the first place. Cockpits had been designed around average measurements—average height, average arm width, and so on. However, no air force pilot was within 15 percent of the average on all ten body measurements. Like the American family with 2.5 kids, the average pilot around whom cockpits had been designed was a statistical mirage. *Every* pilot was **WEIRD**.

The aircraft controls had never been easy to reach. Accidents happened more frequently because planes had gotten faster and their controls more complicated. With less time and more complexity, that extra half an inch required to hit a button or flip a switch went from annoyance to deadly hazard.

Once Daniels convinced the top brass that every pilot was unique (i.e., **WEIRD**), the air force introduced adjustable seats, and the accident rate plummeted.

(There's still room for improvement today. As a five-feet-four-inch private pilot, I sit on three cockpit cushions to see over the nose of the plane.)

Within your **WEIRD** lie your greatest strengths. Unfortunately, parents and teachers try to buff out these quirks. If you have young kids, you probably do the same thing, consciously or not. Teaching kids to fit in is a protective instinct that long ago helped humans survive in small tribes. As adults, we must rediscover our rough edges. To stand out and thrive, hone and highlight every ounce of **WEIRD** you've got. All that talk in the corporate world about personal branding? Forget hiring a graphic designer to pick cool fonts for your website or a consultant to tweak your LinkedIn profile. Building a personal brand means revealing what makes you *distinct*.

Carlye Kosiak was one of our best hires at Google. After rising through the ranks, Carlye is now a global product lead. Did I choose to interview her because of the remarkable accomplishments on her résumé? Accomplishments are table stakes at a company like Google. No, I interviewed Carlye because, besides her impressive work history, her résumé indicated an interest in "recipe tasting in pursuit of the perfect oatmeal raisin cookie." Carlye had the chops to work at Google, but so did fifty other CVs in my stack. She got the interview because her résumé featured a pop of personality the other résumés lacked. In only ten words, Carlye conveyed **WEIRD** (a personal revelation that I wouldn't have known otherwise), **RECKLESS** (taking a risk with the quirky addition that wasn't strictly necessary), **NOSY** (curiosity to learn about baking), and **OBSESSED** (pursuing perfection in oatmeal raisin cookies). Talk about efficient communication (**BRUTAL**)!

Don't run off to add hobbies to your résumé just yet. Being **WEIRD** isn't about saying something "wacky" to catch a hiring manager's attention. It's about being yourself and revealing that self appropriately, both in your résumé and everywhere else. While many people list hobbies on résumés, Carlye didn't write *foodie* on hers. She revealed something specific, fun, and creative about herself. And that was only part of it. Carlye landed the job because the candidate I met matched the colorful clues in her résumé. It wasn't a tactic. It was *her*. *Authenticity* won the role.

To stand out, let it hang out . . . within reason. Figuring out who you are—how you think and solve problems, what you enjoy and dislike, the values that matter most—is essential in (a) deciding what to chase in life and (b) actually catching it. Aiming for average always feels safe, but the results are boring and forgettable. Being forgotten is the real danger in any career. Life is too busy and competitive on this crazy planet for *well-rounded* to make a dent. Get *angular*.

Put yourself in the other person's shoes. When someone plays it cool in a job interview or on a first date, you *know* you're seeing the mask, not the person. The irony is that we crave reality in others yet project a fantasy about ourselves to others. Especially on social media. Then, we wonder why no one pays attention.

Risk authenticity or ensure anonymity.

New Google employees—"Nooglers"—discover that exceptional is expected at the company. These big fish find themselves in an even bigger pond where diligence, intelligence, and competence are par for the course. If they don't make a splash, they sink without a trace.

Think about that intern who worked in your department last summer. They played it safe. Rather than rock the boat, they formatted their résumé according to the guidelines, arrived promptly in the expected business casual attire, and quietly observed every meeting. Where are they now? And what was their name again?

Follow the rules and meet expectations. Pay your taxes and sign on the dotted line. But remember that the unwritten rules we obediently follow to "fit in" aren't rules at all. They're traps, filters to weed out people without the guts to transcend them. Study the careers of notable figures in business, science, politics, or the arts. Breaking with convention is the only rule they consistently follow.

We interpret unconventional behavior as a sign of unusual talent. Jason Feifer, editor in chief of *Entrepreneur* magazine, pointed me to an eye-opening study by researchers at Harvard identifying the "red sneakers effect": we perceive people who dress unusually—wearing red sneakers to a formal event, for example—as higher in status. Because breaking with conventions can theoretically get you in trouble, it follows that someone choosing not to conform must be powerful enough to get away with it.

To be clear, it has to be done with thoughtfulness and intention.

Wearing a wrinkled suit that doesn't fit properly looks accidental. Pairing bright red sneakers with an elegant tux at a black-tie event is obviously a choice. The choices can be meaningful: "Nonconforming behaviors," the researchers write, "as costly and visible signals, can . . . lead to positive inferences of status and competence in the eyes of others." In other words, when someone deliberately breaks the unwritten rules of behavior in a given context, we usually assume they're good enough to get away with it.

It's called a power move for a reason.

As with every **Trait** in this book, there are right and wrong ways to approach **WEIRD**. For example, wearing a black T-shirt to a Michelin-starred restaurant won't convince the maître d' that you're a rock star. Yes, this is the kind of thing rock stars do, but always together with other subtle, contextual details you'll never effectively mimic. If nonconformity signals status, clumsy imitation signals the opposite. We know the real thing when we see it. Stick to what you know and who you are: it's **WEIRD** enough.

According to research, authenticity drives "work outcomes such as job satisfaction, in-role performance, and work engagement." But being yourself isn't just a good strategy for getting ahead. It's good *for* you. Struggling to meet some imagined template—cool, hip, "leadership material"—leaves you feeling alienated and sad. Instead, get comfortable with the discomfort of being yourself. Stop suppressing every impulse and instinct. This liberates enormous mental and emotional energy you can invest in going after what you want. For example, my team at Google was once up for an award we *really* wanted to win. Rather than fill out the submission form with dry details about our project and its business impact, we spent way too much time making a goofy music video. Talk about **WEIRD**.

We all felt so proud of the final product. Unfortunately, we lost anyway. For days afterward, I cringed every time I passed one of the decision-makers in the hallway. I imagined them laughing behind my back: "There goes Jenny Wood, the senior leader who wasted everyone's time on a music video."

Two years later, one of those decision-makers mentioned the incident during a coaching session: "That music video was exactly the kind of thing that sets you apart," he told me. "It was bold and memorable. You do things other leaders wouldn't dare. People notice. It serves you. Keep going."

I took this as confirmation that I'd been too harsh on myself after exhibiting my **WEIRD**. But consider the alternative. What happens if you make a bold, authentic move at work and get pulled aside by your manager for a word? Oof. No matter what you read in some book, getting castigated sucks, especially for doing something that felt smart and genuine. It might not be a music video in your case, of course. The **WEIRD** that gets you in hot water might be speaking an uncomfortable truth about a leader's suggestion, proposing an unconventional solution to an unimaginative manager, or testing an idea without running it up every inch of the flagpole to keep it from dying in committee. The occasional short-term discomfort is real, but I promise you that **WEIRD** pays off in the long run. Push through. Bounce back. Believe in yourself and in what *only you* have to offer.

The so-called safe alternative to **WEIRD** is trying to be everyone's cup of tea. Going along to get along feels perfectly comfortable when you're doing it, but it's so much riskier. The obvious move is easily forgotten. Why make it in the first place? When you put your unique spin on things, from how you speak and act to how you get the job done, you discover kindred spirits, just as banging a tuning fork creates sympathetic vibrations in objects that resonate on the same frequency. **WEIRD** leads to dependable allies, better gigs, and more compatible romantic partners.

You've got a big blue sky to explore. How will you fly the plane if you're squeezed into someone else's cockpit?

PLAY IT HOT

People tell you to play it cool when you're trying to impress. That might work in high school, but planet Earth is slightly bigger. Adding so many people to the mix changes the risk–reward ratio. Weirding out your circle of friends in high school is social suicide. Weirding out someone you met on Tinder is par for the course if you want to find an authentic match one day. Different stakes make for a different game. In the real world, you either stand out or sink into obscurity.

Play it *hot*.

Playing it hot is a strategic commitment *not* to blend in. It's a mindset: *I will bring energy and excitement to every interaction, confident that the benefits outweigh the risks.* Because, in the long run, they always do.

Back in high school, kids strive for popularity, but they'll accept invisibility if necessary. Being invisible is still *safe*. You can quietly get good grades and get into a good college without being invited to every party. (Frankly, getting good grades is easier without a social life.) Everybody knows that the real danger is being noticed for the wrong reasons. If you say something embarrassing in math class, it can spread to the whole school by the end of the day. You're finished.

In your career, on the other hand, you're only finished if you're invisible. If people don't know you're there, they can't send opportunities your way, no matter how talented and ambitious you are. That means no exciting side projects. No promotions. No getting poached by that under-the-radar, high-potential start-up. Sticking your neck out is a risk, but plenty of people who play it safe at work still don't make it through the next round of layoffs. There is no perfectly safe path. All you can ever do in life is maximize the risk–reward ratio.

Look at the LinkedIn profiles of top performers in your profession, and you'll see numerous course corrections in their résumés. These shifts—in role, specialty, and industry—are evidence of their **WEIRD** steering them to the point of greatest leverage. You can always get another job. You'll never rise high in a place that doesn't welcome your talents, perspective, and personality. If you've ever felt that your efforts aren't properly rewarded where you are—job, relationship, city—plant yourself in more compatible soil. The exact same level of performance will translate into better outcomes. It's almost magical.

As a strategy, playing it hot guides you toward welcoming professional environments. Then it gives you the best odds of rapid professional growth. After all, why do some people get stuck while others rise almost as soon as they're hired? *Visibility.* Leaders who don't see you won't think of you for opportunities. Busy people don't consult a database to connect a problem solver with a problem. They try the first name that springs to mind and go from there. The *first* name should be *your* name.

Organizations are opportunity-generating machines. Every day, new stuff needs to be done. New problems need solving. As we'll see in **BOSSY**, a leader's job isn't to solve problems themselves. It's to connect problems with problem solvers as efficiently as possible. Have you associated yourself with solving a certain kind of problem, or at least with healthy curiosity (see **NOSY**) around a given business area? What have you done this week to demonstrate your talents and strengths (see **SHAMELESS**)?

Yes, *this week.* In a large organization, people must be reminded of who you are and what you can do *regularly.* Playing it hot means defaulting to visible over invisible, heard over silent. Being distinct. Being noticed. For example, when you're in a meeting or conference call, speak! Don't just nod along like a wise sage. You add palpable energy by speaking even when you don't say the perfect thing. If your suggestion isn't accepted, it might spark something useful from someone else. If your information isn't correct, being corrected will help everyone else who was also mistaken about that fact. Take the risk and participate. It's always worth the risk to ensure you're noticed and remembered, even if you're the intern.

Especially if you're the intern. You don't have to be an expert to be a valued contributor.

If the idea of speaking up terrifies you, then you *really* need to get **WEIRD**. No book can teach you confidence. You earn it by doing scary stuff like speaking up in a meeting and then realizing you're not dead. The fear and anxiety lessen as the brain sees you miraculously surviving one public vocalization after another: "Hey, I'm cringing, but I'm still breathing—*I can speak in front of other people!*"

Playing it hot extends well beyond business meetings. Whatever your strengths are, leverage them visibly. For example, any work you share within your company (e.g., a useful template you made for client pitch decks) is a résumé that beats any standard CV. Put your name and email on it. A good template can circulate for years and pass all the way to the top of the org. What other strengths can you offer? If you're a natural conversationalist, host a fireside chat for your company with a leader you find interesting. If writing comes easily, stop lurking on LinkedIn and start posting weekly about how you tackle common work challenges. If you're an expert on a technical topic, start a YouTube channel and do some deep dives.

Generating content is only one direction. If you have a talent that lies outside the scope of your current role, start a small side hustle, not to grind yourself into a pulp through overwork but to reveal your capabilities to the world. Showing people what you can do attracts more opportunities to do it.

Opportunity is everywhere, but only a tiny fraction of those opportunities will be right for you. The more you reveal yourself, the more quickly the ideal opportunities will be drawn into your orbit.

Take five minutes and brainstorm five ways to play it hot this week. Look for concrete actions to increase your visibility: sitting in the front row during presentations, being the first to speak up in meetings, disagreeing—diplomatically—with your manager. If the idea of doing it makes you squirm, good—the heat is on.

SHARPEN THOSE ELBOWS

As part of a significant restructuring, first-tier leaders within a Fortune 500 retail company gathered from around the world in London to determine new placements for all second-tier leaders. Through a **WEIRD** "coincidence," some of the more ambitious second-tier leaders arrived in London the same week for *totally* unrelated business reasons. While these sharp-elbowed few didn't have the audacity to crash the actual planning meetings, they made themselves highly visible around the company's London offices and arranged impromptu coffees with the first-tier leaders who were in the middle of deciding their fates.

It takes sharp elbows to rub shoulders. To stand out, put yourself out there. Draw attention. Declare your willingness to tackle opportunities. If your manager asks for extra hands on a project, don't second-guess yourself: "Will I look too eager, enthusiastic, or naive?" Maybe, but so what? **WEIRD** is about pushing through that discomfort, carving a path to your goals instead of waiting meekly for them to drift within reach. They won't.

Being **WEIRD** is about seeking the ideal fit for your abilities and interests. That said, the perfect match is less important early in your career than getting matched in the first place. When you have energy and ambition, try many things without prejudice. This doesn't just raise your profile. It also reveals talent and interests you never knew you had, getting you closer to your own **WEIRD**. You never know what you might enjoy and what you're brilliant at until you've tried it. So raise your hand. Don't overthink it.

If this makes you look eager, good—you are. Similarly, "opportunistic" is another one of those good things that gets a bad rap. Opportunities are *amazing*. We all want them. Unfortunately, our high school–honed egos say the captain should pick us for the team. *Pick yourself.* Seize every opportunity you can. Get comfortable saying, "I'll tackle that!" Whether it's an internal awards program that needs revamping, an AI workstream being formed, or a company baseball team short one short-stop, stake your claim. It doesn't matter if you have no experience. Let *them* decide whether you're qualified instead of disqualifying yourself. If you're given the chance, trust yourself to figure it out.

Do you want sharp elbows? Easy: When you're asked, the answer is yes. When the question is who, the answer is you. Default to *interested, willing, sign me up*. If something needs an owner, own it. What better way to get on your manager's manager's radar?

When you're relatively new to a role, career, or industry, volunteer for three out of four opportunities. Once you've found your professional footing, flip that ratio to one in four to protect your time and energy now that you're better at investing those resources (more on protecting your time and energy in **BRUTAL**). Even once you've solidly established yourself professionally, never close off the flow of possibilities entirely. Leave a little bandwidth open for the juiciest ones.

Yes, you will sometimes overcommit yourself. That's OK. When you're new, others will forgive you for biting off more than you can chew, as long as you're transparent about hitting your limit and needing to scale back. No one expects you to know exactly how much bandwidth something requires before you've ever done it! With practice, you will improve at gauging the time and effort involved in a project.

Elbowing your way into opportunities to help find your **WEIRD**, you'll inevitably encounter challenging situations that require skills you haven't perfected. As a result, you'll work much harder than you theoretically must to earn your paycheck. You may even make embarrassing mistakes in front of peers. *Still worth it.* The world's most successful people weren't given a secret map of future opportunities: "Look here, that BlackBerry thing is going to be a big deal in two years." Instead, they dug holes in likely places, failing repeatedly until they struck oil. That's how life works. Industries and professions change. If you don't stake claims to new territory, your odds of finding a gusher are always zero.

If you are searching for a role within your current company, consider that many job opportunities are announced publicly only as a legal requirement. The people making the call draw on a bench of talent they're always mentally assembling. Leaders keep lists, whether for new projects, maternity leave backfills, or succession planning. You go after these opportunities not by submitting your résumé to open roles—too late by then!—but by regularly declaring your interests and demonstrating your abilities (more on this in **SHAMELESS**). Whatever your interests and talents, advertise them. Let peers, managers, and industry connections know (a) what you're good at doing, (b) what you're eager to improve, and (c) what you're just plain interested in trying. When something opens up, you'll be much likelier to hear about it in time.

MAKE YOUR MARK

Starting in the Middle Ages, papermakers used watermarks to prevent counterfeiting. To this day, fine paper still reveals a trademark when held to the light. Photographers, illustrators, designers, and filmmakers use digital watermarking techniques to ensure they receive credit for their work, an increasingly difficult challenge in the age of AI.

Watermark your work even if you don't have an artistic bone in your body. This isn't to prevent colleagues from using what you've made but to help those who like your stuff find its source.

It's great when someone at your company uses your expertly crafted slide deck or budget spreadsheet as a template or draws on data from an internal report you created in a presentation. We want them to know how to find your brand of **WEIRD** next time. Label anything you create with your name, contact info, and names of your collaborators. If you're contributing to an asset, let everyone who uses it know you played a role.

For example, if you write a strategy document, put your name and title somewhere visible. You never know where something like that might end up. Don't force the curious to check "File > Owner" (if the software even allows it) to find out who made something. Make it easy. Likewise, if your team collaborates on a slide deck, put everyone's names and photos on the cover slide to make it easy for people to spot you in the hallway. The typical title slide says something like "Q1 Quarterly Business Review." No names, no owners. People want to know who you are when you give a presentation. This isn't a distraction but a help. What distracts an audience are unanswered questions. People look at the calendar event to deduce your identity from the invitee list instead of paying attention to you. Save them the effort.

Watermarking isn't weird, it's **WEIRD**. (Remember, the Traits appear in bold to distinguish them from their original, negative connotations.) Think of it as *branding*. If you love movies, you want to know if *this* movie had the same cinematographer as the similar-looking one you loved last year. You might want to watch all the movies in their filmography. Similarly, if work is being completed on an impeccable renovation in the neighborhood, the architect's sign on the lawn saves time and effort for other homeowners needing such help. The architect isn't bragging. They're being *useful*. If you do good work, people will want more of it. Stop being precious and help them find you.

Of course, this presumes you're making work worth sharing. How do you make your mark before reaching the point that your accomplishments speak for themselves? Create a memorable introductory snippet four or five sentences long summarizing who you are and what you can offer. Then, put that vivid micro-memoir on your desktop as a text file or in your note-taking app. From now on, paste it into your correspondence whenever you're dealing with someone new.

As a rule, preparing assets like these before you need them helps break bad habits—like being self-effacing—by reducing the friction involved in taking a new approach. If you tend to keep your head down, preparing a short bio is an easy way to reduce the cognitive and emotional effort of sticking your neck out. All you have to do is copy and paste. For example, when Maya learns that a leader in operations needs volunteers for an interesting new project, she doesn't do what she normally does (wait for someone to think of asking her to volunteer, which never happens). Instead—before she can psych herself out—she throws her hat in the ring with her preprepared bio:

> *I'm Maya, and I'm on the marketing team. I've been at Minnesota Metalwork and Manufacturing for two years after spending five in sales in another industry. My strengths are influencing through storytelling, improving processes, and program management. On my team, I'm known as the go-to "ideas" person who gets carried away when brainstorming. I'd love to be considered for the project.*

Your bio doesn't have to be complicated or flowery. Just explain who you are, what you've been doing, and what you can offer. Preparing a bio in advance is handy when the urge to hide makes it difficult to raise your hand.

Personal branding isn't complicated. It's just scary, especially early in your career when you can't point to a long list of wins. When in doubt, lead with enthusiasm—no asset is more in demand in a large organization. In the spirit of **WEIRD**, stick to showing real enthusiasm (a) because leaders can spot phony enthusiasm a mile away and (b) because your excitement will lead you toward more of the work you care about. As we'll see in **OBSESSED**, enthusiasm fuels effort. How else will you knock that golden opportunity out of the park?

TRAIT TRAPS

Every chapter of this book closes with **Trait Traps**: guardrails to flag your attention when a strength threatens to become a weakness. Beware too much of a good thing.

Pay the fine

The first Nike Air Jordan was mostly red and black in defiance of regulations requiring basketball sneakers to be at least 51 percent white. When the NBA fined Michael Jordan $5,000 for violating that rule, Jordan—and Nike—celebrated. Nike had already agreed to pay the fine on Jordan's behalf with the intention of turning the NBA's decision into a marketing bonanza: "On September 15, Nike created a revolutionary new basketball shoe. On October 18, the NBA threw them out of the game. Fortunately, the NBA can't stop you from wearing them." In short order, all fifty thousand pairs were sold—covering the fine easily—and a billion-dollar brand was born. Talk about a red sneaker effect.

Newton's third law of motion states that every action has an equal and opposite reaction. When a comedian offends part of their fan base with a joke, they do so in the hopes that the rest will laugh and that more people who appreciate edgy humor will be drawn in. Growth entails loss. It's never a question of avoiding fines but choosing the ones worth paying.

The next time you're tempted to get **WEIRD**, ask, "What's the fine, and is it worth the expense?" If you're going to speak up, do it with the understanding that you may not get a positive reaction. If an intern proposes an idea in a meeting with a bunch of VPs, that's a risk. It might impress three leaders and irritate three others. The intern may receive a compliment *and* a reprimand the same afternoon. How does the intern decide? By calculating the value of that internship if no one remembers them at the end of the summer. Stay quiet if all you need is the company's name on your résumé for the three-month stint. Speak up if you want to stand apart from the fifteen other interns chasing the same full-time role in the fall. Pay the fine.

Honestly, though, the most common risk of **WEIRD** is just the sting of embarrassment. Be honest with yourself when calculating possible fines. Imagining the worst this way is a defense mechanism to keep yourself small and safe. Going after what you want with wild courage isn't safe, but neither is standing still. (See **RECKLESS**.) When you're unsure how to play it, roll the dice and bet on yourself.

Be your (best) self

WEIRD doesn't mean unpleasant, abrasive, aggressive, or rude. We've all had that "friend" who insults people and calls it being honest. All they're doing is unleashing their hurt and resentment. Being yourself is vulnerable *and* generous: you risk letting people know how amazingly unique you are.

In short, this **Trait** is about highlighting your strengths; it's not a license to talk nonsense or go for shock value.

On the first day of seventh grade, when I was new to the school and didn't know a soul, my English teacher, Ms. Howard, asked us if we had any questions. Insecure and desperate for a laugh, I asked, "Are you a virgin?"

What. On. Earth.

No one laughed. They just cringed in embarrassment until my teacher mercifully went on with the class. I knew I was not being my best self even as I said the words. That afternoon, I coincidentally spotted Ms. Howard in the greeting card aisle at the grocery store. Mustering courage, I approached her. They were the ten longest steps of my twelve-year-old life, but I managed to stammer an apology. She graciously accepted it.

Being genuine isn't about saying strange or offensive things to get reactions. It's about trusting in your authentic reactions instead of second-guessing yourself out of desperation to fit in. When I say put yourself out there, I mean give of yourself. Share assistance. Share what might be useful or interesting with other people. Be the most helpful person in the room. Make a habit of this generosity, and people will look to you for more of what you've got. We don't start contributing once we become leaders. We become leaders because of how we contribute.

Lapsang souchong is a black tea famous for its intensely smoky aroma and flavor. Literally and metaphorically, it is not everyone's cup of tea. Lipton lovers shun it. AriZona drinkers probably wouldn't qualify it as tea in the first place. However, for a devoted minority, it's a beloved favorite. Like so much in life, there is no objective "better" and "worse" here. Lapsang souchong is just not for everyone. Neither are you.

WEIRD is so powerful because being yourself fearlessly is a powerful act of self-love that *also* helps you make your mark. However, it isn't enough just to be yourself. You must *stand up* for that true self. Defend it. Seize opportunities when they drift in reach. The next chapter asks, Why *not* you? Does going after what you want in life make you . . . **SELFISH?**

WEIRD
Win as you, or lose as "who?"

- **Play it hot.** Unlike high school, the real world is too crowded and competitive for us to wait to be noticed. Be visible, sit in the front row, diplomatically disagree with your boss, and share your best stuff with the world.

- **Sharpen those elbows.** When starting in a role, career, or industry, say yes to at least three out of every four opportunities.

- **Make your mark.** Prepare a four-to-five-sentence intro to quickly tell others what you can offer, then paste it everywhere. When you make something, take credit so people know where to find more of what you offer.

- **Pay the fine.** Instead of avoiding mistakes entirely— and stifling growth—write off the negative consequences of smart risks as the cost of doing business.

- **Be your (best) self.** Stand out by highlighting your strengths, not going for shock value.

2

SELFISH

Be your own champion

> **Selfish**
>
> **(adj.):** concerned excessively or exclusively with oneself.
>
> **Selfish redefined:** The courage to stand up for what you want.

Amelia, a leader at a large bank, has always been supportive of co-workers and direct reports. She's the colleague who tells you to apply for that unlisted role the minute she hears about it. The one who clues you in to your manager's priorities in approving promotions. The one without whom navigating your organization would be significantly harder. Amelia's a born helper. The kind of person you want in your corner. The only person who can't count on Amelia's unwavering support is Amelia herself. She's selfless to a fault.

Usually a top performer, Amelia once let a side project distract her from her primary job function long enough to earn a less-than-stellar quarterly evaluation score. This score hovered just above performance-improvement-plan territory. While the tone of her manager's feedback was encouraging, the gist was "get your eye back on the ball."

This distracting side project hadn't stopped Amelia from contributing but from investing enough effort in making her contributions visible.

In your career, it isn't what you do that matters. It's what your managers *think* you're doing. This may seem unfair, but managers aren't mind readers. Part of your job is letting them see that you're doing your job.

It wasn't that Amelia didn't understand the importance of visibility. She'd recently let a junior colleague take the lead communications role on a project because he was up for promotion and could use the boost in profile. Leaders at the bank credited the person communicating on behalf of the team—via weekly emails and updates in leadership meetings—with most of the effort regardless of how the work had been divided.

Amelia faced a dilemma. Once again hoping to help a colleague, she had planned to encourage her direct report, Maeve, to run comms on another project. Now Amelia's own profile needed a lift. Could she raise her hand for this opportunity instead? Seizing something she'd mentally earmarked for a team member felt . . . selfish.

When Amelia shared her moral predicament with me, I repeated what my dad always said: "Unless you're the lead dog, the view never changes." The dog at the head of a sled team works harder but gets to watch the evergreens rush by. The rest of the dogs see butts. Nothing but butts. (Odd thing to keep telling your kids, but maybe it instilled my leadership spirit.)

Amelia's manager needed confirmation that Amelia was once again focused on her primary role. How would that happen if she kept pushing others into the limelight? Amelia needed to be **SELFISH** to safeguard her career.

IN DEFENSE OF SELFISHNESS

We value selflessness for evolutionary reasons. Self-sacrifice makes sense in a tribe. If you risk your neck to put out your neighbor's fire, they'll return the favor when a spark lands on your house. This communal mentality is still heavily reinforced in modern times: "You can eat your birthday cupcake only if you have enough for the whole class."

Don't get me wrong: sharing with friends and family is beautiful. The problem is that our "tribe" is much bigger now than back in the Ice Age. If you give *everyone* a leg up at your own expense, you'll get trampled. This doesn't feel like a moral victory when it happens, either. When someone else walks away with what you wanted without a fight, you experience resentment, regret, and even anger. What you don't do is feel pride in your own generous nature. In moments when you give too much and defer your shot to others, that anger may feel like it's directed at the other person, but deep down, you're mad at yourself for not going after that opportunity when you had the chance.

Being **SELFISH** doesn't mean seizing everything you can like a treasure-hoarding dragon. It means championing your agenda at least as strongly as you champion the needs of others. Fighting for yourself just as enthusiastically as you fight for your friends and colleagues. In movies, the protagonist's selflessness and modesty inspire a helpful mentor to raise them up. In real life, people help those who are busiest helping themselves. Allies flock to your side only once you're going somewhere. Show them your success is inevitable; they'll help you get there faster. We all want to join a winning team.

Call it **SELFISH**. Savor the word. It helps spot the opposite impulse, that insidious guilt you experience around doing something for yourself: Skipping that meeting because you need thirty uninterrupted minutes to catch up on actual work. Missing the kids' bedtime routine to prioritize a much-needed yoga class. Delivering the presentation even though five of you contributed. The guilt is natural. Caving to it every time is self-defeating.

Do the people around you put you and your needs ahead of their own as consistently as you do theirs? Every boss you've ever had has put their career ahead of yours. Of *course* they did. Sure, a great boss will care deeply about your career development. I've always prioritized the careers of my direct reports. But never above my own!

SELFISH is protective, inside and outside your career. Leave if you're miserable in your relationship and see no way to improve things. You owe something to your partner, but *you owe more to yourself*. Don't sacrifice your happiness for someone else's. **SELFISH** is a crucial **Trait** that transforms personal *and* professional results.

"But wait, Jenny," I hear you saying, "isn't selfishness the *problem* in this crazy world?" The media tells us selfishness is rampant, but it's not. The poor behavior highlighted on social media and the nightly news is the exception that proves the rule; most people are happy to help others most of the time. Maybe not complete strangers, except in the case of the die-hard selfless, but certainly the people we know. Humans are *hard-wired* to care about their colleagues and, of course, their friends and loved ones. Brain scans show that a threat to someone we know lights up the same brain region as a threat to ourselves. The researchers call this the "blurring of self." In other words, the mind struggles to distinguish between our needs and the needs of the tribe. When we act callously, it's usually because we don't know the person yet. It takes very little, sometimes just a "Hey, can you believe the coffee maker's still broken?" to shift someone into "known" territory.

Selflessness is a powerful instinct and, if unchecked, a harmful one. Being **SELFISH** ensures that our needs are met even when our "tribe" extends to thousands of people across our personal and professional networks. Start by acknowledging that *you* are as important as anybody else in your life. Does that feel uncomfortable? Point to someone more important than you are. If your answer is "my child," tell me: How can you act as a loving, patient caregiver if no one takes care of you? Also, does your kid need a miserable martyr as a role model?

You *matter*.

If you're qualified for and interested in an opportunity, don't let it go to someone else without a fight. When is it your turn? When do you get your shot? Moral righteousness is a drug. The one thing to stop pursuing is the high of self-sacrifice. You'll regret it later. Also, stop worrying that others will see you as pushy. Large projects at companies stall out because there are too many cooks in the kitchen, with each employee so worried about stepping on anyone's toes that *nobody* takes the initiative. Step up and get it done. This isn't about stealing glory. Communicate transparently about who's doing what and make sure everyone doing the work gets their name on any documents, emails, or slide decks. Just stop waiting for collective action. Ensure your manager will back you up, then make awesome stuff happen. The credit will sort itself out once success has been achieved.

It doesn't seem like you would need techniques for being **SELFISH**, but this is hard for most of us. (That's why the truly self-obsessed find it easy to snatch more for themselves.) It still takes deliberate effort for me to prioritize my needs. For example, when my husband and I told my New York–based in-laws that we were moving to Colorado with the kids, I felt nauseated with guilt. My hands shook. Though I don't cry easily, I blubbered like a child. We knew the distance would devastate these wonderful grandparents, and we both wanted to make them happy, but our needs took us elsewhere. Though it was necessary, it *hurt*. Looking after your needs at someone else's expense usually does. Do it anyway.

Selfishness isn't just hard when dealing with those we love. The other day, I got into a Lyft to the airport. The car was *freezing*. However, I shivered silently instead of asking the driver to turn on the heat. The truth is, I didn't want to make the driver uncomfortable, even though I had every right to avoid frostbite. As I struggled with this bout of selflessness, I noticed a sign on the back of the driver's seat: "PLEASE LET ME KNOW IF YOU NEED ANYTHING. CHARGER? MUSIC? AC OR HEAT?" That lovely, generous man! Finally, I felt comfortable asking for a little warmth. Isn't it amazing that I felt I needed permission to make a reasonable request? **SELFISH** is about giving yourself permission to pursue your agenda.

At the beach, my son, Ari, who was four then, wanted to play with one of several bright, colorful buckets lying nearby. Older kids were using one of the buckets to build a sandcastle. The others were just sitting there. Ari asked me to ask the kids if he could borrow one, but I encouraged him to ask them himself instead.

"No, Mommy," he pleaded. "*You* ask."

"You can ask for what you want, sweetie," I said. "I'm not going to do it for you."

No one was using those extra buckets, but Ari still had to muster his courage to ask. The kids agreed without looking up from their work, and Ari went on to build a hell of a sandcastle.

Why push my son to do the asking himself? Because **SELFISH** is a muscle. It gets stronger with practice. Ask for what you want repeatedly, and the asking will get easier.

Ask for the raise.

Ask for the promotion.

Ask for the date.

If these feel too heavy, start lighter. Ask your spouse to pick up the kids this afternoon. Ask a coworker to review your presentation. Ask the waiter for a menu substitution. Start small and build strength through repetition.

What are you still afraid to ask for, and why?

SAY YES TO THE BIG, NO TO THE SMALL

For most of my career, I was lucky to work at a place where I felt highly valued and respected. Unfortunately, many companies strategically leverage selflessness by laying guilt trips on their employees: *Work hard, stay late, never see your loved ones, don't complain, don't form a union, and one day you, too, will get that promotion and see your equity vest.*

There are valid reasons for trends like "quiet quitting." Society needs solutions. However, the solution for *you* isn't underperformance. That's soul killing. Nor is the solution demonizing your boss, who is just another human being under similar pressures. We're all part of a capitalist system here, and that system drives us all a little bit (or a lot) crazy. *Your best bet with a systemic problem is a systemic solution.* If your boss quits on Wednesday, a new one with the old agenda will arrive on Thursday. If you change jobs without changing your approach to work, you'll end up in the same situation by the end of your first ninety days. The problem (for you, not society) isn't your boss. It's your boundaries. Or lack thereof.

There's much more on boundaries in **BRUTAL**. For now, get **SELFISH** by *saying no to the small*. What's small? There is no payoff in being the eighteenth person to reply all to the "Happy Birthday, Larry" thread. There is no advantage to you in quibbling about a minor point in someone else's presentation. There is no promotion waiting for the person who attends every weekly status meeting without fail. Not long ago, all managers had administrative assistants. The good assistants were treasured for protecting the boss's time, energy, and attention. Today, we must be **SELFISH** and protect ourselves. Do so aggressively. Be a bulldog around your calendar and to-do list.

We say no to the small so we can *say yes to the big*. What's big? For example, raising your hand for this year's marquee strategy project or your boss's top Q2 business priorities. Tasks like these may be intimidating and involve lots of work, but they will bolster your résumé and put you in the room with higher-ups. Say yes to these opportunities and then knock them out of the ballpark. My friend Amelia from the start of this chapter did this, and it brought back that high evaluation score she'd been chasing.

Think of this not as a binary choice between big and small work but as putting your thumb on the scale. If you can shift your efforts even 10 percent away from low-payoff, time-wasting work toward high-impact, high-visibility work, the effect on your career will soon be impossible to miss.

You've likely realized that being agreeable often invites more responsibility but *not* more authority. There is always one person on a team everyone else counts on. When the group needs something done, they'll expect that person to do it. Without complaint, he—or, more often, she—will shoulder the administrative burden despite the reality that tasks like taking notes during meetings, planning accommodations for off-sites, or decorating for holiday parties aren't rewarded. This is NAP work: not actually promotable. (Credit to my mom for coining this phrase.) Leaders praise a can-do attitude but don't promote can-doers who do nothing big.

Don't NAP at work.

Most managers aren't monsters exploiting the unwary. When you say yes to every piece of NAP work that comes your way, you show your manager *through your own actions* that you have unlimited bandwidth to tackle mundane tasks. True or not, they start to think you have nothing more important on your plate. If you did, you'd say no more often. Wouldn't you?

Olivia, a senior product manager at a large consumer packaged goods (CPG) company, was asked to communicate employee satisfaction results at the company's town hall. She crushed it. In the following months, Olivia sensed her success at the podium had tipped her brand toward people projects and away from the core business. (People projects matter, but for a leader at a competitive CPG company, they quickly become NAP work.) Together with her manager, Olivia brainstormed a meaty, revenue-oriented project to hang her hat on at her annual review. She didn't want to be pigeonholed as the "people-project person." Being **SELFISH** means tracking how you are perceived by others and shaping that perception in your favor. This is personal branding where it counts.

You may be familiar with the expression "If you want something done, give it to someone busy." The "busy" people in a company are uncomfortable appearing idle. But the most valuable work usually doesn't *look* like work. Thinking, planning, visualizing, estimating, brainstorming, and strategizing all look like sitting still and staring out the window, but they are the core functions of a leader. (As we'll see in **OBSESSED**, we share the results in concrete form as an email, doc, or presentation, but that represents only a fraction of the time spent window gazing.) When someone bustles around hectically all day, no one can accuse them of slacking off, but no one suspects them of thinking much, either. We expect less noise and more signal from leaders. A hectically bustling CEO is a sign to sell your shares in the company.

The hardworking packhorses shoulder every load because they can't face the discomfort of saying no, even when they have more important things to do. Rather than defend their agenda, they give their time away. Then they wait in vain for concrete recognition. Sorry to break it to you, but since the invention of the internet, no one has ever been promoted for being ultra-responsive on email. You've been prioritizing the wrong things.

From now on, when presented with the small, say no firmly, with a brief explanation and a smile. Never apologize or equivocate:

"Do you have five minutes to hop on a call?"

"No, I'm heads down in Q4 planning right now."

"Can you lead logistics for our November off-site?"

"No, my bandwidth is maxed out with the customer satisfaction project."

(I've included more scripts for saying no to different kinds of asks, including meetings, projects, and favors, as well as tips for backing out of or renegotiating deals at **wildcouragebook.com/resources**.)

Stop waiting for your manager or colleagues to magically know your bandwidth. They don't know how busy you are or how effectively you allocate your time and energy. Sighing is passive-aggressive, but it isn't no. Nor is grimacing. Only no means no (more on that magic word in **BRUTAL**).

Saying no to the small *feels* risky, but it doesn't *look* insubordinate or lazy to others. It actually makes you look like you're working on valuable contributions to the team.

PLAY TO WINN: WHAT I NEED NOW

Navigators who refuse to course correct at sea might reach landfall, but probably not where they intended to arrive. Always remember that you can change your goals midway, even when it's not ideal for others. You only get one life. The **SELFISH** question you must ask is: What do I need *now*?

For example, let's say you petition hard for a new role, get it, and then discover that you and your partner are expecting a baby. Uh-oh. Now you're legitimately apprehensive about managing twice the business travel with a newborn at home. Yesterday, this was a fantastic opportunity. Today, it's a problem.

Ambitious people in this scenario will feel pressured to follow through rather than let people down or lose face. For example, I spent two years pursuing the volunteer role of cohead of Google's Colorado office. However, when I was offered the opportunity, the role represented too much work for too small a payoff. Declining a role I'd fought so hard to get felt scary, but I realized it wouldn't serve me as I'd originally thought. Though the subsequent conversation was tough, I still remember how wonderfully **SELFISH** it felt to walk away from a mountain I no longer wished to climb.

It may not feel good to disappoint others or back down from a challenge, but it remains absolutely, 100 percent OK—ethically, practically, and strategically—to change course. Yes, you told leadership how much you wanted the job. Yes, you did several rounds of interviews. Yes, people may feel frustrated about the wasted effort or the awkwardness of approaching rejected candidates. That's life. Believe me, when your bosses' personal situations change, they don't hesitate to change course, even at your expense.

We pin our resistance on others, but more often, **SELFISH** is an internal struggle. We are our toughest critics. A few years ago, becoming a lawyer made sense to you. Now, it no longer does. Does it matter that you've passed the bar exam and have an offer from a top firm? The law is no longer your path. This doesn't make you a dilettante. Just human. The sooner you learn to balance the things you're trying to get against each other, the happier you'll be. Goals are great, but your original goals may have faded in importance for reasons you never could have predicted when you set your sights on them. Don't ignore your intuition and call this stubbornness "discipline." While you might need a pep talk to keep going, it's also possible that you've changed. Find the wild courage to move on to what matters now.

To align yesterday's ambitions with today's circumstances, play to WINN: **What I Need Now.** Just as your long-term vision informs your day-to-day decision-making, your day-to-day experiences should shape your vision. Changing course often feels selfish because your plans inevitably involve other people. However, everyone's needs and desires change over time. What you wanted may no longer resonate. As a strategy, WINN means continuously coordinating your short-term experience with your long-term vision.

Similarly, revisiting an agreement when circumstances change isn't "going back on the deal." It's just **SELFISH**. For example, the English band Pink Floyd hired session singer Clare Torry to improvise vocals for the track "The Great Gig in the Sky" on *The Dark Side of the Moon*. Convinced she hadn't done a good job—more on impostor syndrome in **SHAMELESS**—Torry took her thirty-pound fee and went home. She didn't even know the track had made it onto the album until she saw her name in the performer credits on the record sleeve.

The Dark Side of the Moon became one of the bestselling albums of the 1970s. Certified platinum fourteen times, it has sold forty-five million copies to date. Torry found the original arrangement unfair in light of the album's success. The band hadn't told her what to sing. *She* had created those legendary vocals. Didn't that mean she deserved a song-writing credit—and a share of the enormous royalties?

It wasn't selfish in the negative sense when Torry took the band to court. Just smart. Likewise, the band was smart to settle out of court for an undisclosed sum and give Torry her songwriting credit. Life is fluid. So are the deals we make to navigate it. Are there any arrangements in your life worth revisiting?

- Last year, you did the laundry. This year, your partner's firm went fully work from home while you're still commuting five days a week. WINN: renegotiate the split of household chores.

- You said no to a third date. Four months later, you're wondering if you made the wrong call. WINN: call them and book date number three if they're still open.

- Two years ago, you set your heart on becoming a manager. After a short stint to cover a leave, you've decided management isn't for you. WINN: find another ladder to climb.

To embrace a What I Need Now (WINN) mindset, consider your scenario from an outside perspective. For example, you've covered three full-time positions for the same pay since a series of layoffs at the organization. It was a rocky patch, and you were grateful to be spared the ax. However, the company's fortunes rebounded months ago. Why hasn't the company replaced the other two roles yet?

"I'm just happy to have a job," a little voice says. Fair enough, but imagine a friend came to you with the same situation.

"What do you need now?" you ask your friend.

"What I need is a raise," your imaginary friend replies, "a title that reflects my responsibilities, and two direct reports. The numbers easily justify it."

"Sure," you reply, "but a deal's a deal. You agreed to take on the additional work. I believe the legal term here is 'no backsies.' Your only option is to push yourself to the limit until you burn out and quit. I'm sure that's the outcome the company wants, too."

If a friend had the same problem, you'd tell them to make their case to leadership. We hesitate to "go back" on a commitment made under very different circumstances only when the problem is our own. Just look at the crazy thoughts we have in these situations:

- Sure, the company's doing better, but for how long?

- Sure, I need more money to pay my rent, but so do James, Mia, and Camila—where are *their* raises?

- Sure, my title doesn't match my responsibilities, but I like working here—it doesn't matter what my résumé says or how much I'm earning as long as everyone knows how important I am.

Show up for yourself—you deserve an advocate! Stop asking, "Why me?" Why *not* you? (You can download scripts to negotiate for a raise, promotion, or starting salary at **wildcouragebook.com/resources**.)

Success requires a steady flow of energy and enthusiasm. If you rarely experience that flow, pay attention. Do you still want to succeed at this particular pursuit? Incredible things become possible when you make a habit of releasing goals and ambitions—not to mention personal and professional relationships—that no longer matter. When your destination is no longer relevant, don't let angst about time and money spent trick you into continuing a fruitless quest. This is the "sunk-cost fallacy," the natural human bias to throw good money after bad. What's gone is gone. Aim for the WINN. Ask yourself, "What do I need now?"

While you care deeply about the people you love and will help the occasional stranger in need, you also have things you want to do in your finite life. Things you want to experience and accomplish. That's your agenda, and *it's just as worthy and valid as anyone else's.* Stop deferring to those with fewer hang-ups about being **SELFISH**.

SMART START

While good managers recognize and reward hard work with raises and promotions, bad ones are like black holes, absorbing everything you give them and still demanding more. When you work for someone like this, every small mistake is a catastrophe. No feat of skill, effort, or persistence is acknowledged . . . let alone rewarded.

You'll never catch anything on a hamster wheel. Run fast, run slow—you're still going nowhere. Rather than chase validation you'll never catch, find something better. Every time you seek a role, prioritize your direct manager. That person will affect your career trajectory and overall job satisfaction more than any other factor, including, in many cases, the company itself. A manager can make your life fulfilling or miserable—I've experienced both kinds.

The START framework flips your mindset as a job applicant from "hire me" to the far more **SELFISH** "wow me." START stands for Style, Thoughtfulness, Attitude, Responsiveness, and Transparency. It helps you evaluate a manager to ensure they will support you in achieving your ambitions *before* you take the job. To play a game you can actually win, one where your hard work is rewarded, prioritize finding the right manager.

Style. A hiring manager emailed me during an internal hiring process with the subject line "Stuff!" She wanted to update me on interview-related details. Another applicant might have found "Stuff!" too vague, but to me, it suggested a friendly and informal communication style similar to mine. Pay attention to these telling details in terms of not only how the manager communicates but also thinks and makes decisions. It isn't about a "right" style but compatibility.

Clues to style can be found throughout the interview process. What you can't observe firsthand can be gathered from mutual contacts or other people on the manager's team when you meet them. Never commit to a role without conducting a thorough vibe check.

Thoughtfulness. Managers who charge like bulls after business objectives with zero consideration for other people might serve the company's needs but rarely those of direct reports. Avoid them.

Being thoughtful includes being present. Someone who starts texting during your interview isn't present. Is the manager respectful of your time? A good listener? Do they value your thoughts and opinions? Are they *there* with you in the interview or a hundred places at once?

One manager showed up eight minutes late to our thirty-minute interview. This made me anxious and affected my performance. Then she ended our discussion without leaving time for me to ask questions, putting the final nail in the coffin. Without the willingness to think of others, you can't lead effectively.

Attitude. I once found myself interviewing for two roles simultaneously. This allowed me to compare the two managers' body language and word choice. One was optimistic and eager, almost bouncing out of his chair. He wanted to "tackle challenges together." He said he needed A players to "fundamentally shift the tech industry." Ambitious stuff—the discussion left me fired up and grinning. (More about the effect of positive energy in **MANIPULATIVE**.)

The other manager, dour and depleted, harped on negatives: "The work-life balance drains some people because we work across multiple time zones," he said. Good to know, thanks. "These three people are the ones you actually need to keep happy," he said. I'll keep that in mind. "They're pretty demanding," he added. Sounds fun.

Yes, the second interviewer was being honest by identifying headwinds. However, his body language and tone conveyed burnout and disenchantment. A manager's job is to coach and inspire you. Appreciate the unvarnished truth when you get it, but don't sign up for a burned-out boss out of gratitude for their honesty.

Responsiveness. During one job search, the hiring manager responded immediately whenever I pinged her: "Quick question," I'd write. "Absolutely, I'm here," she'd reply within a few minutes. These responses indicated how she would show up for me down the line.

Responsiveness is incredibly important when you're stuck on an important project, need a roadblock removed, or crave general guidance. Your boss assigns the work *and* helps you tackle it. If they're never there for you when you need to meet them, you will find everything a struggle. Evaluate responsiveness and availability from the beginning. How does a manager spell love? T-I-M-E. It's unlikely to improve once you've taken the gig.

Transparency. Your manager gives you the feedback you need to evolve into your next role. If they can't or won't tell you what you're doing right and what still needs work, you'll struggle to grow into the next opportunity.

A while back, I received a verbal offer for an internal role. Because I was on the brink of promotion in my current one, I told the hiring manager I'd accept only if we agreed she would put me up for promotion in the upcoming review cycle. This would require the support of her own manager.

Her response was refreshingly straightforward: "I emailed my manager about the promotion," she said. "Let me pull up that conversation." She read the entire exchange, which indicated their mutual support for the idea. *Whoa.* Most hiring managers keep their cards close to their chest. This manager's transparency affected my decision more than the promotion prospects.

Approach any important new relationship, from business cofounder to romantic partner, with a smart START. Being **SELFISH** means insisting on the allies you deserve.

TRAIT TRAPS

Grow the pie

As with every other **Trait**, you must strike a balance with **SELFISH**. One thing you want to avoid is bringing a binary "me or them" energy to the situation, whether it's a negotiation, a sales pitch, or your job as a whole. Not only is this attitude poisonous to your mental and emotional well-being, but it's also obvious to everyone around you. We've all experienced a hard sell. When somebody sees you as a means to an end, you can feel it in your gut, even if you don't know why.

For example, don't focus on salary alone when negotiating a job offer. Ask for something else you'd appreciate: extra vacation days, for example, or a signing bonus, or the right to work from home one day a week. There are areas other than compensation that might be easy for the company to grant but won't unless you ask. Expert negotiators call this widening your ZOPA: zone of possible agreement.

Seek to grow the pie instead of simply your slice. Find a way for everyone to get more of what they each want, and they will be even more flexible and gracious with you later. All this takes is a little patience and openhearted discussion. If you need someone else to cover work emergencies over the Christmas rush because that holiday is a big deal in your family, don't go in guns blazing. Ask around first. You may discover that one of your colleagues prioritizes Thanksgiving and would be thrilled to trade holidays. We all have different needs. Instead of defaulting to *me*, look for the *we*.

Second-dog advantage

As I said earlier, Dad used to tell us the same thing regularly: *Unless you're the lead dog, the view never changes.*

Personally, I took that to mean I should be driven and tenacious in everything I did. When something feels a bit out of reach, reach *harder*. Being the lead dog meant blazing my own trail. In trying to fit in with the pack, people pleasers please no one, least of all themselves.

But there's a flip side. You can get carried away. You can become so swept up in grinding your way to the top that you neglect life's other priorities. There's an undeniably nice view from the top, but life has many peaks, personal and professional, and the unsparing pursuit of one inevitably comes at the expense of the others. So be honest with yourself: Do you really *care* about being the lead dog? It's one thing to *want* the pole position more than anything but hold back out of misguided selflessness. Don't do that. But what if you're happy following? Turns out Dad himself was:

"What do you *mean* you never wanted to be the lead dog?" I asked.

Dad had shocked me by mentioning this in response to a social media post I'd written celebrating his advice for Father's Day.

"As a real estate developer, I liked being lower in the rankings," he replied. "I was fine not being the dominant player in Denver. The top real estate firms made more money, but we always did well. You can make a nice living picking up other people's crumbs! I know I said otherwise, but my thinking has evolved."

I'd struggled with Dad's lead dogma as a kid, but it grew on me. Today, I know I *like* leading at work. But that's me. Plenty of people have no interest in blazing trails, and you might be one of them. That's great: this book is about courageously pursuing what *you* want, not somebody else's definition of success. There is no "right" level of ambition. Seek your own happy place regardless of title or position.

Success means finding the right position *for you*, one that optimizes your return on investment of time and energy. Economists describe the "second-mover advantage" of companies entering a new category late. Thanks to the category pioneer, the work of educating consumers about the product is already done. Many mistakes have already been made. You're coming at the problem fresh while the lead dog is running on fumes. If you can execute on the promise better, you can be successful with less effort.

Many dominant brands commonly believed to be first weren't. For example, Oreos arrived after Hydrox cookies, even though most people think Hydrox did the copying. Likewise, Glaxo's Zantac wasn't the first treatment for ulcers on the market, but it quickly became the bestselling one. Customers knew similar drugs existed, so Glaxo didn't have to waste marketing money convincing ulcer sufferers that an effective treatment existed. Instead, they could trumpet the fact that their version had fewer side effects.

The rewards of being second dog might not be as big, but neither are the risks. It's an easier path that may also be more enjoyable. Just be honest with yourself: Do you prefer the safer approach, or are you suppressing your desire to lead because you've been taught to defer to the needs of others? It's OK to reach for the top spot. It's also OK to seek a healthy balance, leading in some areas and following in others.

Many behaviors labeled "selfish" are rational self-interest in action. Unlike the overly cooperative members of *Colobopsis explodens*—ants that explosively self-destruct to protect the colony from invaders—it's natural for members of *Homo sapiens* to look out for their individual interests.

Sometimes, looking out for yourself in healthy, appropriate ways can still bring up intense feelings of guilt and shame. To free yourself, you must learn to frame that discomfort as a positive indicator of personal growth. In the next chapter, we're going to get absolutely **SHAMELESS**.

SELFISH
Be your own champion

- **Say yes to the big, no to the small.** Avoid low-payoff work to tackle more of the high-value, high-visibility projects that will accelerate your career. Do 10 percent less NAP work (not actually promotable).

- **Play to WINN: What I Need Now.** Don't hesitate to abandon goals and renegotiate deals when circumstances render them obsolete.

- **Smart START.** When job hunting, prioritize working for a manager who will see your value and support your ambitions. The right manager can be more important to your career than any other factor, so evaluate their style, thoughtfulness, attitude, responsiveness, and transparency.

- **Grow the pie.** To get what you want, find ways for everyone else to get more of what they want. Expand the ZOPA (zone of possible agreement) in any negotiation.

- **Second-dog advantage.** It's inefficient to always seek the lead position. Outside of a few key areas, draft in another leader's wake to save time and energy.

3

SHAMELESS

Find your swagger

> **Shameless**
>
> **(adj.):** insensible to disgrace.
>
> **Shameless redefined:** The courage to stand behind your efforts and abilities.

Grandma Lila was **SHAMELESS**. At eighty-eight years old, she agreed to be a bridesmaid in my wedding, and she couldn't have cared less how she compared to the others half a century her junior. She was cranking out push-ups at one point—we have the video. **SHAMELESS?** At four feet ten and ninety pounds, Grandma was *unstoppable*.

Grandma's credo was "No is just an opening offer." She sold annuities for a living—retiring as CEO of a financial services firm at ninety-two—and brought as much cheerful and unapologetic shamelessness to selling as she did to everything else she did in her long, rich, and vibrant life. Whenever a customer told her no, her eyes gleamed. That meant it was time to *sell*.

When my husband, Jon, and I moved back to New York City after he earned his MBA, we spent a few months on Grandma's pullout couch to save money while we looked for apartments. We'd eat dinner with her every night while she imparted wisdom with characteristic sweet bluntness. We soon needed that wisdom, because Jon's company informed him he would be part of a major layoff right after starting his new job. Last in, first out—the usual drill.

When we told Lila the news that evening, she got that gleam in her eye.

"No is just an opening offer," she reminded us. "Don't sign the paperwork."

Jon sighed, as practically anyone would when confronted with . . . seemingly unrealistic advice like this from a beloved elder. *Just refuse to be let go?* But he kept his poker face on.

"I don't think it works that way," Jon said. "A layoff is a one-sided thing. They say, 'You don't work here anymore.' I say, 'OK.'"

That's when *Grandma* sighed, as practically any successful octogenarian CEO would when their advice isn't given the appropriate consideration. She knew very well that Jon wanted to do what *everyone* does when they hear no: leave with their dignity intact. While she didn't say the words, she certainly thought the obvious response: *Who has time for dignity when they're sleeping on a couch?*

"It works any way you can *make* it work," she said. "You both want something. You want this job because it's always easier to find one when you have one. Your bosses want stuff done even though they can't afford to pay you. So you each have something to gain."

Jon nodded.

"Sure," Grandma Lila continued, "taking no for an answer would be more comfortable, but the discomfort will pass. Get your ego out of the way and find a compromise. What's the worst that could happen? They've already let you go."

Jon relented. After all, he had nothing to lose but pride—which is not something you're brimming with when sleeping on a sofa, anyway. He returned to his boss with a counteroffer: "How about I stay on at 10 percent time—and pay—while I find another job?"

To his surprise, they immediately and gratefully accepted the deal. Jon could keep his position while job hunting—and use the company printer for résumés. In return, the company got some important stuff done. It wasn't perfect, but both sides got something out of the deal. Lo and behold, the company moved Jon back to full time when the crisis passed. The whole ordeal took a couple of months. Jon's dignity? Barely dented.

The moral here isn't that you, too, can get yourself unfired. Jon's experience was a fluke. Grandma Lila's lesson was more profound: don't let shame shape your decisions.

IN DEFENSE OF SHAMELESSNESS

When was the last time you felt ashamed at your job? The answer may not spring to mind, so I'll put it another way: When did you last beat yourself up over a mistake at work, or otherwise worry about what people would think about something you did, said, or wrote?

Is the answer . . . right now? Are you ruminating at this moment about a late project or imperfect performance evaluation even as you (try to) read this book? I wouldn't be surprised. "Shame" may seem abstract, but we all know what it's like to get in our own heads because of a miss, mistake, tricky relationship with a colleague . . . even a strange look from the boss. "What did *that* mean? Are they mad at me?"

This is shame at work. It's the feeling that you're not OK as you are. Shame manifests as anxiety, internal criticism, embarrassment, and stress, taking a constant toll on our mental and emotional bandwidth. To others, our feelings of shame can come across as self-doubt and lack of confidence. When we sense this happening, it can lead to a shame spiral. Oof.

Shame is an appropriate emotion at times—we'll get to that. But it can easily become a toxic burden that serves no healthy purpose, dragging us down and preventing us from performing well, let alone enjoying our lives. For many of us, shame becomes reflexive. We lean into feelings of shame in *anticipation* of failure rather than as a result of it.

Have you ever struggled with self-promotion? In a meeting, a colleague delivered a "shameless plug" for a resource document she'd created. After performing a valuable service for everyone in the room, she apologized for drawing their attention to it. Why?

Think of it this way: Doing things your way is **WEIRD**. Letting people know you're proud of how you do things is **SHAMELESS**. The next time you feel the urge to apologize for sharing something you've made, try this: "I'm proud of a resource I created and excited to share it with you."

Psychologists identified impostor syndrome in 1978. At a time when women were achieving new heights in the workplace, many told their therapists they felt phony, as though they didn't deserve their positions. These professional women, many of whom were the first executives at their companies, experienced the feeling that they'd fooled everyone about their abilities and accomplishments, even when they knew on an intellectual level that they hadn't. If anything, they had to be overqualified to end up where they were despite rampant sexism in the corporate world. The facts didn't matter. They felt like impostors.

Since the 1970s, more research has shown that impostor syndrome affects all kinds of people, regardless of their gender, sexual orientation, age, experience, or accomplishments. It's something we're all prone to experiencing. Accolades don't cure it, either. If anything, external recognition makes it worse: "If the Nobel Prize committee knew the truth about me, they would never have considered me in the first place. . . ."

Impostor syndrome is just one manifestation of shame, an emotion that holds us back and keeps us small, long before that middle-of-the-night call from Sweden about our Nobel Prize.

Fear. Blocks. Us. From. So. Much.

How powerful are these feelings? One colleague kept a charcoal nylon backpack under her desk, packed tight. Because she never opened it or took it to the gym, I asked her what was in it. (Why? See **NOSY**.) She fessed up: "Personal effects. Knickknacks. Framed pictures. You know, for my desk." Though my colleague had been hired months earlier, she was so worried the company would realize its "mistake" in hiring her that she couldn't bring herself to unpack.

When you keep your bag packed—literally or metaphorically—you limit your performance. You can't do your best work when you're convinced that you don't belong, that some authority will deem you unworthy and force you out. It can become a self-fulfilling prophecy. When fear and shame hijack your amygdala and send you into a panicked state, you physically can't be as creative and productive as you usually would.

Because positive affirmations and even objective facts are useless against impostor syndrome, you have only one option: acceptance. The feeling is real. It isn't going away. Time, experience, and accomplishment won't cure it. Being **SHAMELESS** means working through feelings or even working *with* them. Start by unpacking the bag. It's a change of mindset. Rather than treat shame as something to push down and ignore, heed its message. Use shame as your compass. It flares up when you put yourself in challenging situations where the outcome really matters. You feel it around intelligent and capable people who impress the hell out of you. That nagging sense that you don't belong is your intuition telling you that you're exactly where you *need* to be if you want to grow.

Now, stay there.

In the Jewish community, we call the ability to go somewhere you feel out of place—and do what you need to do anyway—chutzpah. Chutzpah is Yiddish for swagger, gall, audacity, *nerve*. As perennial outsiders, we've always relied on our chutzpah to survive. When people treat you like you don't belong, you have no choice but to give that approval to yourself.

Audacity—being **SHAMELESS**—is a crucial survival skill in life and business. Everyone needs chutzpah to thrive in a big, messy, competitive world. You never know how you compare with others if you don't push past the shame and put yourself on the line. For example, you will never *know* where you sit in the rankings for that juicy opportunity if you don't go for it. It's easy to psych yourself out, but that's just shame talking. Maybe you don't match another candidate's experience on paper, but maybe you exceed them in diligence, care, patience, availability, and enthusiasm. Being human, we focus on our flaws and perennially downplay our strengths. Others don't see us through the same lens. It's *always* possible that you're the very best person for the job.

You'll never find out if you don't act like it first.

SHAMELESS begins with owning your strengths. Embrace and highlight what you can offer. Ask yourself: "What's a struggle for others but easy for me? What am I passionate about? Where have I made the greatest impact?" If these questions bring up negative self-talk, flip those defeatist thoughts on their head. No experience? "I bring a fresh perspective." Don't know the internal politics yet? "I have an unbiased view of the players." Every weakness is a strength from a different perspective. It's on you to figure out how to leverage everything you've got. I call these **Power Assets**.

Take the time to label and memorize your three most distinct and valuable **Power Assets** for sharing with mentors, bosses, and anyone else who can influence your career or help you get what you want. This will be your **Power Portfolio**. Memorize it.

Whenever you sit down for an informal one-on-one with a leader—when you're seeking a mentor, for example—you'll get asked what you're working on. This is an opportunity to segue from current projects to your **Power Portfolio**: "I'm preparing reports on the success of the new sales initiative, which is great because I love finding patterns in data." We hesitate to write down our strengths because *looking* like we've prepared in advance is embarrassing, but that's shame rearing its ugly head. Why wouldn't you prepare for an opportunity?

Personally, I am unashamed to say that I'm good at "people leadership," "stakeholder influence," and "building programs from start-up to scale." Those are my most valuable **Power Assets**. Identifying them has helped me in three ways:

1. I can align my strengths with other people's needs.

2. I make more progress doubling down on my strengths than shoring up my weaknesses. As a rule of thumb, I put 75 percent of my energy into the former and 25 into the latter. Years of the opposite ratio didn't work nearly as well.

3. Knowing my **Power Assets** makes it easier to tell others. Whenever I meet people who can give me a leg up, I let them know why they should. Is sharing my **Power Portfolio** with others **SHAMELESS**? Good!

Say you walk out of a performance review where your manager said you were strong on A, B, and C and need to develop D. The rest of the day, all you can think about is "I'm no good at D." Congrats, you're like every human ever born! It's a natural response but also an unhelpful one. Lean into your strengths from now on. Double down on A, B, and C. Put at least three quarters of your attention on what's working. When you get home after your review, don't complain to your partner or friend about needing to improve D. Share your strengths on A, B, and C. The next day, ask your manager for more projects that align with those strengths. Let everyone know about them. Give yourself a **SHAMELESS** plug. There's no time to wait for the perfect moment to shine. Tell people what you're good at, or they'll never know.

Not all **Power Assets** are created equal. One mentee, Martina, came to me with three:

- Communication

- Organization

- Supporting others on launches

These are OK but in need of tweaking. For example, people skills matter, but hiring managers want to know how you will solve business problems. That's what their boss will grade *them* on. Diversify your **Power Portfolio** just as you would any portfolio of investments. Aim for at least two hard business skills, though the proper framing can put an edge on even the softest strengths. "Organization" and "supporting others" are vague, which makes them impossible to prove. In Martina's mind, they felt "safe" to share. Unfortunately, they left out the real-world business capabilities she brought to the table. This was shame telling her, "Don't overdo it."

Here's how we tweaked Martina's list:

- Executive communication

- Project and program management

- Go-to-market strategy

Same ideas, different word choices, higher impact. **SHAMELESS.** (You can download a simple exercise to create your **Power Portfolio** at **wildcouragebook.com/resources**.)

In this chapter, you will bring a new dose of swagger to your life. This can be as simple as forwarding a happy customer's email to senior leadership—why *not* cheer a win? People should know who you are and what you can do. They may need what you can offer. It's not bragging— it's sharing! The goal is to advocate for yourself as aggressively—and shamelessly—as any Hollywood agent does for a favorite client.

No more apologizing for who you are and what you can do. If you don't act like you already own the place, you never will. Here's a layup to get you started: Count how often you write "I'm sorry" in emails each day (e.g., "I'm sorry this took so long," "I'm sorry to bother you"). Then decrease that figure by 50 percent. Add tally marks to a sticky note on your desk every time you do it, including verbal apologies in meetings. There's always an alternative: "Sorry I'm late" can be "Thanks for your patience."

REFRAME THE SHAME

"Shameful" is subjective. Shame is an emotion generated internally based on our beliefs and values. Something that shames a person from one culture might inspire a sense of triumph in someone from another. The feeling emerges (or doesn't) depending on the stories we tell ourselves about our lives. The morals of these stories are passed along to us by parents, teachers, and peers early in life. Though you may no longer agree with some of these attitudes intellectually, you can't help but experience some shame when you transgress your oldest programming (i.e., rules like sit still, don't make a fuss, and do what you're told).

To get better at **SHAMELESS**, try telling the story differently. Reframe the narrative to release the shame preventing you from getting what you want. New story, new emotions.

That said, sidestepping shame through storytelling isn't always desirable. Shame is an important emotion. A pang of guilt—"I shouldn't have yelled at my kids just now"—can motivate us to do better next time. However, most of us carry far too much shame about small things like speaking up or asking for our fair share. That kind of shame does nothing more than burden us and keep us playing small.

One of the reasons shame can be so paralyzing is that we feel—and remember—negative emotions more than we do positive ones. This is a well-known cognitive bias. For example, a single bad experience at a restaurant can be enough to sour your opinion of the place despite having had five memorable meals in a row. The brain evolved this negativity bias to keep you safe. It emphasizes what goes wrong—or might go wrong—because there are no do-overs when dealing with hungry lions on the savanna. Once you understand this bias, you can consciously right-size your response to difficult situations: "Forgetting to attach the file before sending that email made me *feel* like hiding under my desk, but that's just my brain trying to keep me safe—people forget attachments pretty often. Life goes on. I'll send a quick follow-up email with the missing file."

If screwing up at work leaves you wanting to find a dark cave, acknowledge to yourself that shame is a normal and healthy reaction. OK, you didn't live up to your standards in this situation. Next, devote five minutes to listing concrete actions that would have prevented the mistake from occurring. For example, if you skipped something important during a complicated, repeatable process—doing the company payroll, launching a website, etc.—creating a checklist can ensure you never miss that step again.

Applying shame's energy to finding a solution brings relief. Shame is healthy when it motivates positive change. Taking action tells your brain that you're solving the problem. It's the lingering shame—"What kind of idiot needs a checklist to complete a job application? I suck!"—that has to go. Remind yourself there's nothing wrong with removing friction from a task, building safeguards against mistakes, and otherwise increasing efficiency. It's called being a pro.

To reframe the shame, use a tool I call **Truth and Tales**.

1. Write down the basic facts of what happened. This is the **Truth** you're working with.

2. Next, write down the **Tale** you're telling yourself—and how that story makes you feel.

3. Reframe the shame. Write down a **SHAMELESS** interpretation of the event. This essentially means writing a version that sticks closer to the facts, skewing positive or at least neutral.

4. Watch the shame melt away.

For example, the Truth might be: "I misspelled a word in an important email." The Tale? "Every recipient of that email now thinks I'm incompetent." Is it possible you have unrealistic standards? Concrete actions like reading important emails out loud will help catch errors. However, if you can't shake off the sting of an occasional typo, you have an unhealthy, self-defeating attitude toward perfection. Reframe the shame with a new, more accurate narrative: "Mistakes happen to everyone, and my emails are cleaner than most at this company." With repetition, your emotional responses to occasional mistakes will soften.

I'm as susceptible to Tales as anyone. For example, my manager once moved our Monday one-on-one to Thursday. On Thursday, he pushed it to Friday. Those are the facts. My Tale? "I'm getting laid off. That always happens on a Friday. I'm sure our HR person will be in the meeting, too." Naturally, I checked the HR person's calendar. Busy at the same time, huh? As I suspected.

A fellow leader, Tara texted me Friday morning: "I know there's a lot of change happening in your org—hope it's not impacting you!" Aha! Confirmed. If she texted me that, she'd clearly heard something. Now my head was spinning. Why hadn't I been more focused at work? Why hadn't I pushed my team harder? How did I end up here? So much shame!

After an hour of pre-layoff prep—moving family photos to my personal laptop, etc.—I shook it off. My Tale was just that: a fabricated story. The Truth was, my team had been delivering outstanding, high-impact work lately. Putting the story aside, I spent the remaining time on *actual* meeting prep, stocking our running document with wins, brainstorming topics, and business updates.

Good thing I did.

"Thanks for your flexibility this week," my manager said at the start of our call. "I've been vomiting all week."

Tales can become self-fulfilling prophecies. You start underperforming across the board, so caught up in futility and resentment that you deliberately sabotage yourself. Focusing on the Truth solves the problem. Even if it doesn't, even if your Tale is true, assuming the worst doesn't lead anywhere productive. Passive-aggressively underperforming because of shame only reinforces bad habits and undermines your self-esteem. In fact, if we're really good at telling Tales that feature us as the tragic hero against a hostile universe, our anxiety and resentment can build to the point that we sabotage our career more effectively than any capriciously vindictive boss.

The next time you run face-first into the facts, tell a Tale only if it keeps you motivated and focuses your attention on positive actions. Otherwise, stick to the Truth. Facing reality isn't always fun, but it has a remarkably energizing effect. That's because we believe what we tell ourselves.

BIG TALK

It's "drama queen," not "drama king," for a reason. Misogynistic terms undermine men and women. Women suppress their feelings for fear of stirring up any of that dreaded "drama." Men play "strong and silent" for the same reason—how embarrassing to lose one's masculine cool . . . even if the building is burning down.

When you hear a little voice telling you to chill out instead of speaking up, interrogate that thought. Yes, if all you want is emotional validation about a tough day at work, seek it from friends and family, not the CEO. However, if an important fact about work should be shared but might make people uncomfortable, speak it anyway. When you're **SHAMELESS**, you stand behind your opinions and beliefs, confident that what matters to you will matter to your colleagues and peers.

Shame and embarrassment always vote against direct communication of the truth. The waiter brings lukewarm mashed potatoes to the table, and you eat them rather than "make a fuss." Enough of that. Send. The. Potatoes. Back. If you don't pay for your meal, the restaurant won't hesitate to make a fuss. The waiter will shamelessly chase you down the block. So why are you willing to eat cold potatoes when you're paying for hot ones?

I once conducted a goal-achievement assessment online that, in part, indicates how bold people are. Of the seven thousand respondents across ninety countries, 67 percent asserted, "I ask for what I want." Yet only 36 percent said, "I'm comfortable asking for a raise," and, believe it or not, only 23 percent would send the potatoes back. (You can take the assessment here: **wildcouragebook.com/quiz.**)

How do we get past this nearly universal programming to get **SHAMELESS**? "Acting as if" is a powerful tool for silencing the inner censor. Next time you want to ask for something, *act as if* you're the kind who wouldn't hesitate. Picture that confident, unflappable colleague who speaks their mind without hesitation—and gets away with it. Ask yourself: Would *they* raise this issue now? If so, how? Often, this simple shift in perspective immediately clarifies things.

Next, if you're going to say something, say it clearly. Don't dance around the issue, don't get quiet, and don't ramble. This is shame softening your words in an attempt to hide your truth. If you tend to hem and haw, record your next call, play it back, and note every vocal tic. How many *um*s can you count? *Likes*? A manager once told me he watched the recording every time he presented. That seemed like a waste of time to me . . . until I became a regular guest on podcasts. I'd listen to every episode. Twice. It made me better.

Big gatherings are another opportunity to work those mouth muscles.

Think *hands high.* Get in the habit of asking questions during the Q&A portion of *everything,* whether it's your organization's quarterly town hall or the school PTO meeting. It helps if you sit close to the front, signaling you're invested and paying attention. Now, open that big mouth. Asking the *first* question builds swagger. Leaders notice and appreciate those who speak up first. It not only conveys boldness but also decreases their anxiety that no one will ask anything. Be the person who helps them.

Ask without hesitation and use as few words as possible. Think *confidence* and *clarity.* If it helps, write your question beforehand to avoid the "mini monologue at the mic" people tend to deliver before getting to their point. Whatever works for you.

Joining a public speaking organization like Toastmasters or taking a speech class can help, but all the knowledge in the world won't give you courage. Sometimes *ahs* and *likes* are innocent filler words. Other times, they might be an attempt to avoid rejection or cushion others from difficult truths. When given something tough to say—negative feedback, for example, or a raise request—we "build up" to what we need to say with a big bowl of word salad.

It's normal to feel uncomfortable before an awkward conversation. I sure do! Whether delivering bad news or asking for what you want, you can't help but want to delay. Or to layer on so much verbal camouflage that the truth gets buried. Tell the truth.

In a meeting, your colleague says something that rubs you wrong. You feel hurt, invalidated, and frustrated. Fearing an awkward conversation, you keep it to yourself, silently stressing about every encounter with them for weeks, months, or years. Bizarre? *People do this every day.*

I once felt wounded by a vague sentence in a colleague's email. Suddenly, I felt anxious whenever I had to speak to her. Finally, I mustered the courage to ask her to clarify and, as it turned out, I had completely misinterpreted. With the awkwardness out of the way, we became close confidants. To this day, she is one of my favorite people.

Why drag things out due to embarrassment? Avoiding the awkward conversation leads to missed opportunities, unnecessary tension, and soured relationships. They say that sunlight is the best disinfectant. Speak up and get right to the gist, squashing that shame. All that throat clearing only builds dread. A manager I had once talked for seven minutes before sharing my performance rating. The rating was fine, but seven minutes of hell preceded the good news. If you don't have the guts to come out and say what needs to be said, that's OK, but don't tell yourself you're being kind or gentle to the other person. Delay is selfish—and not the good kind!

The next time you have something to say, brace yourself, take a deep breath, and get right to the point. Share the ugliest part within the *first ninety seconds*. Any shame or discomfort you experience will pass, followed by immense relief.

- To a peer: "I feel like I'm pulling a lot of weight on this project. Can you start owning comms while I continue to design the slide deck?"

- To a direct report: "You're having a high impact on the corporate rebranding project, and I know you're passionate about it, but we have too many cooks in the kitchen, so I'm moving you off it."

- To your boss: "I'm on late-night calls three days a week, which isn't sustainable. I must reduce that to one or have other teammates take on some of my projects."

Another avoidant tendency is imprecise word choice. When a peer criticized an aspect of her data analysis, Daria, a pharmaceutical exec, replied, "My hair was a bit blown back by your feedback."

What does that mean? Was Daria upset, sad, frustrated, demotivated, confused, surprised, or invigorated? There's no shame in expressing an actual feeling or emotion at work. It's better to resolve an issue quickly and correctly than dance around it with euphemisms. In this case, Daria's peer had never heard that expression before and had no idea Daria meant she was offended. Choose your words bravely.

Opening your big mouth benefits everyone: "If you're meeting with an executive and you're not asking for something, you're wasting their time," my friend Akiko, who works in communications at Amazon, says. As a former executive myself, I agree completely. Whenever someone set up a time to meet, they usually wouldn't get to their ask until the last two minutes of the thirty-minute meeting. So I'd spend the first twenty-eight minutes fretting because I didn't know how to help them resolve their issue. Eventually, I'd start getting paranoid, wondering whether I'd missed the ask because I hadn't been paying attention.

Whether someone needs money, head count, the removal of a roadblock, or a simple decision, hesitancy doesn't increase the odds of a yes—it just leaves both sides drained. Executives *expect* people to ask for things. Removing roadblocks is their job. Asking for what you want at the beginning of the meeting isn't greedy; it's efficient. Don't bury the lede.

Shame doesn't care what you're saying or asking. It just wants you quiet, inoffensive, invisible—"safe." Opening that big mouth habitually builds that **SHAMELESS** muscle. The more you do it, the easier it gets and the bigger your life becomes.

When Alexis, a colleague, transferred to the Boulder office with her husband and toddler, they didn't know a soul. Despite being new in town, however, Alexis mustered the courage to email the company's Boulder Parents mailing list, inviting a ton of strangers to celebrate her daughter's third birthday. Doing this took guts, but seventy people, including me, attended the barbecue. Alexis and I have been friends ever since.

SHAMELESS is miraculous.

Now, don't just blab or drone. *Communicate.* A colleague of mine regularly delivered the most compelling presentations in our entire org.

No matter what this particular colleague brought to the podium, I had no problem following along. Even if my attention wandered for a moment, or if I entered the presentation halfway through, it never took more than a few seconds to catch the gist. When others gave presentations, I usually found myself lost, whispering, "What are they talking about again?" This colleague just had a *natural* talent for conveying information.

At least, that's what I thought. When I saw her slide notes before a talk, however, I realized that she prepared for each one by meticulously color-coding her notes. Words in gray were spoken in a hushed tone, orange words were loud, purple went to a higher register, and so on.

"We have a natural tendency to stay flat," she explained later. "The colors are like musical notations for me. As in a presentation, music is relative. If you want the music to feel loud in one part, you must get soft first. The colors remind me to switch things up to hold the audience's attention. They create an arc that leads from a dynamic opening all the way to a thrilling conclusion."

If you're going to speak the truth, make sure everyone hears it.

CHEER EVERY WIN

Growing up, we're told that "bragging" (i.e., taking pride in your efforts) is shameful. Depending on where you grew up—parts of Asia and Latin America, for instance—your hesitation to share might feel even more acute. But in the real world, the cream doesn't rise to the top—it's lifted. No one cheers your wins if you don't do so first. Likewise, our schools instill the idea that good work is automatically celebrated with certificates and awards. Show up, make the grade, and you'll get a pat on the back. Honestly, how many trophies have you received since the day you started paying your own rent?

Get **SHAMELESS** and cheer your wins. If doing this feels uncomfortable, look at yourself in the mirror and say, "It's OK to express pride in my work. It's OK to tell others what I've accomplished." If Harry Styles enjoys listening to his own albums—which he says he does—it's cool to cheer every one of your own wins, macro *and* micro.

Macro win: "I hit my $500,000 sales goal."

Micro win: "I signed my first repeat client."

Macro win: "I hired a team of ten people."

Micro win: "I left a full five minutes at the end of the interview for the candidate to ask questions instead of my usual two. Kudos, me."

Celebrate progress, and it will beget more progress. My colleague Manuel Altermatt translated a Spanish phrase that sums it up: "Chickens don't just lay eggs. They also cluck." Get clucking! Tell your manager, peers, and loved ones what you've accomplished. Don't you want your kids to know you're out there kicking butt and taking names? The day after I sold my book proposal, I got my son ready for the day, took him to school, waited for the bell to ring, and then whisked him off to a water park to celebrate together. That'll teach him hard work pays off!

Spread the good news with *pride*, the best antidote to shame:

- "I'm proud of how the customer responded to the solution I delivered."

- "I'm proud of how I presented to our partners."

- "I'm proud of how I acted on your constructive feedback."

- Various scripts and strategies to tastefully self-promote are available at **wildcouragebook.com/resources**.

Your company didn't hire you to be invisible. It's your *responsibility* to share your work with your team and the organization. Cheer at every opportunity. Get **SHAMELESS**.

Simultaneously, shut down self-deprecation and negative self-talk. When a highly competent writer handed me one of his emails to cut down, I felt deeply insecure about my effort: "I'm always bad at cutting," I told him. "I probably let you down here. It's just not my skill set." Shame ("I'm bad . . ."), shame ("I let you down . . ."), and more shame ("not my skill set").

Instead, I should have said, "You're so good at writing that almost everything felt crucial." The second sentence conveys the same message—"I didn't cut much"—without shaming myself. Plus, I made him feel better, not worse.

You bring these habits to your management style. If you downplay and undersell your own efforts, your direct reports must feel truly invisible. Cheering every win means assigning credit liberally wherever it belongs, highlighting your team's accomplishments. Our brains weigh misses much more heavily than hits. Overcoming this bias takes deliberate and consistent effort—actively seek opportunities to praise your team for their efforts. Aim for a five-to-one positive-to-negative feedback ratio. You may have heard about "toxic positivity," but this is really rare to find in practice. Far more often, the overall slant from bosses is negative. While you can take the cheering too far, the upper limit is much higher than you think. People need tons of positive feedback to perform at their best.

Email, chat, and other online communication tools are obvious channels for celebration but not necessarily the most effective. A meeting with senior leaders, even on another topic, is a great opportunity to call out your win. Extra points if you squeeze a cheer into a town hall meeting. Raise your hand to ask a question of a leader and quickly mention a great metric about your team's recent accomplishment. In a meeting, calling out a win seizes attention and also helps bring everyone up to speed. It never fails to warm the room (see **MANIPULATIVE** for more on warmth).

The best part about being a manager is that *you never have to steal an ounce of credit*. You receive full points when your team wins. A leader's most valuable trait is bringing out greatness in others.

Want to self-promote tastefully, not shamelessly? Simple: when your team knocks it out of the park on a project, email them to thank them for the work, whether you're their manager or just the project lead. Subject line: "Amazing work increasing chocolate ice cream sales 22 percent year over year!" Copy your boss and your boss's boss. In fact, cc any additional senior folks who matter for *your* career. Thank *down*; cheer *up*. Subtle and effective. Plus, whenever someone sends a reply all, that powerful, impact-conveying subject line gets driven home a little further.

Your boss isn't psychic. In fact, leaders *like* to hear about the accomplishments of people in their organization. One of the reasons it feels otherwise is known as *pluralistic ignorance*. This is the assumption that our feelings don't align with everyone else's. Most of the time, everyone thinks the same thing everyone else does—and is convinced they're the exception. Pluralistic ignorance explains why nurses as a group rarely acknowledge the stresses of the job—and think they're alone in feeling so overwhelmed. It's why corporate board members aren't vocal when they're concerned about the company's strategy—they think everyone else on the board is on board. When we believe we're the minority opinion, we keep that opinion to ourselves. This is why you can simultaneously be happy to hear about a direct report's accomplishment yet be convinced that your manager doesn't want to hear about your accomplishment.

Your manager has several times as much going on as you do: everything on your plate and the plate contents of however many other direct reports. Bang the drum, not because your manager isn't intelligent or doesn't care but because their brain can't see and retain everything you do as easily as you can from where you're sitting. They have a lot more to worry about and optimize for than you do as an individual contributor. They're not incompetent. It's just math. Seven direct reports means seven full plates to manage. Also, leaders have the same negativity bias rattling around in their heads as you do in yours. If you don't consistently communicate all the great things you're doing, their brains will naturally focus on the problems.

Start here: Every Monday, send a **SHAMELESS** email to your manager with last week's accomplishments and this week's priorities. You can note objective highlights (a milestone achieved) and subjective ones (a glowing client testimonial). Above all, deliberately use *proud*: "I'm proud to say we achieved three out of four of last week's priorities." You *should* be proud! You worked hard last week. Show the world. And get specific. Don't write, "We're making progress on the design work."

For example, someone in the graphic design department might write:

Last week's accomplishments:

- *I'm proud of the updates I made to our seven-page brand guidelines for our chocolate truffles product.*

- *I'm right on track at 80 percent completion on our spring in-store marketing campaign.*

This week's priorities:

- *Get full alignment across three stakeholders in marketing and art direction on spring launch dates.*

- *Compile document on chocolate industry trends, positioning, and brand experience of competitors.*

Writing this up shouldn't take more than fifteen minutes of your Monday morning. Still, you'll feel the urge to skip it—that's shame at work. Don't listen to it. Another advantage of doing this weekly is having everything prepped for your performance review. One less headache—who remembers in March what they did back in January?

When the time does come for your performance review, it's worth the additional effort to go back and ensure that each accomplishment bullet you include demonstrates ROI, but not the kind you might be familiar with:

- **Role.** What part did you play?

- **Objective.** What were you aiming to do?

- **Impact.** What did you accomplish?

For example: "I led three technical specialists (**Role**) to address the top twenty-five customer troubleshooting issues. Filed five bug and feature requests with engineering to remove customer pain points (**Objective**). Of these, two were implemented, leading to a 12 percent increase in customer satisfaction year over year (**Impact**)."

This isn't practical for a weekly email, but when the stakes are high, **ROI** delivers a huge ROI. As we saw in **SELFISH**, it's not what you do but what your manager knows you're doing. Let your manager know!

TRAIT TRAPS

Don't be a robot

Self-promote, but do it tastefully. Keep impostor syndrome in check, but don't be obnoxious. Stay positive when a project goes off the rails, but don't be oblivious. When a project fails after months of effort, don't become a manic cheerleader when everyone else is still licking their wounds.

SHAMELESS doesn't mean clueless. As with every other trait in this book, achieving the right balance is everything. I've included suggestions and guidelines here, but you'll have to fill in the blanks through observation, especially if you're a touch socially awkward like me. You can always have too much of a good thing.

There's no rush! Turn the shamelessness dial gradually, and pay attention to the results you get. How do the people who matter to you respond? If your approach works, spread your wings even further. If not, dial it back or try something else. Don't use the advice in this chapter as a license for bizarre, outrageous, or offensive behavior. Instead, see it as an invitation to reveal more of your *best* self.

Of course, you can know where shame is holding you back and still struggle to overcome it. In that case, a gradual approach is still your best bet. If cheering wins in front of the whole team feels too bold at first, at the very least, stop downplaying your strengths and otherwise sabotaging your efforts.

I hear stuff like this too often: "I know there's way too much text on this slide, but . . ." You had the option to cut it. You chose to keep it, so explain your reasoning instead of presenting yourself in the worst light: "Granted, there's a lot of information here, but the third column is so interesting I wanted you to see it in context with the other two. . . ."

Self-deprecation is a defense mechanism, one that's obvious to everyone else in the room. Also, it isn't funny, even if people laugh. They're laughing because they're uncomfortable. Silence is always better if you can't find a good thing to say about yourself yet. Let your work speak for itself.

Own your mistakes

SHAMELESS means being willing to make mistakes to learn. If you adopt the habit of speaking up and making a splash, your career trajectory will tilt toward the vertical, but not just because it puts you on management's radar. Hiding is safe. Nothing you say can ever be refuted if you never say anything meaningful. If you speak up boldly, on the other hand, you'll be visibly, irrefutably wrong now and then, especially at first. This is important, because mistakes are how you grow. You'll learn the right approach by taking the wrong one. Just make sure to learn from every error. But screwing up doesn't stop there.

Some people who talk a good game when things are going well clam right up when things go south. A crucial part of **SHAMELESS** is the willingness to acknowledge and repair your mistakes. If you have the guts to speak your opinion with candor and cheer your victories in public, you ought to take that same brazen approach to pointing out where you've messed up, what you'll do about it, and how to ensure the same mistake won't happen again.

We're all familiar with that hot flush of shame after making a doozy of a mistake. Have you ever clicked send on an email only to realize you've sent it to precisely the wrong person? Oof. Now that client knows exactly how low you're willing to go on price. There's no walking it back. The heat in your chest in moments like these can make you want to hide under your desk.

Don't. We can fix this. When handled properly, mistakes can work in your favor. (We'll go deeper on this idea in **RECKLESS**.)

People react in all kinds of counterproductive ways when they screw up—as though *anyone* gets through a single day without a few mistakes. We get angry, dismissive, or even passive. Sometimes, the shame is so hard to bear that we will ghost rather than face minor consequences.

"What happened to Alex?"

"Who, the intern? He accidentally deleted a file and never came back to the office after lunch. Doesn't he know we have backups?"

No matter the mistake's severity, the worst thing you can do when you make one is deflect, downplay, or otherwise dodge. You might "get away with it" here and there, but this strategy is a career killer over the long term. Usually, these "subtle" maneuvers are *entirely* transparent to managers and peers. However, even if everyone around you is clueless, sidestepping responsibility removes the opportunity to learn from your mistake and help others avoid making the same one. If it's easy for an intern to accidentally delete a mission-critical file, keep the intern and fix the process.

Owning mistakes isn't easy. Good bosses respect this behavior, but lousy ones may not. That's OK—as we learned in the last chapter, working for a lousy manager is a career dead end regardless.

If you're going to talk a good game, you'd better play one, too.

Swagger helps you stand out and raises the team's energy level, but execution and effort are requisites. If you don't follow through on your big talk and outsize presence, people will catch on. Sooner or later.

This book's first four chapters are about making yourself a priority. That's important, because we're all told in one way or another to toe the line and fit in. It takes effort to break out of that old thinking and put yourself first. That mindset change is just the beginning, however. To see results, you must focus on the quality of your work, too.

Your current job may not be your life's ambition. In fact, you may hate everything about it—and everyone you work for or with. If you expect to achieve your ambitious goal, however, you'd better start thinking of your current job as a *part* of achieving that ambition. It's a rung on the ladder, even if just by keeping you fed and housed while you work on what's next. Never wait to be acknowledged before delivering work that *demands* acknowledgment. Go over and above if you expect to rise. To get ahead, you'll need to be a little **OBSESSED**.

SHAMELESS
Find your swagger

- **Reframe the shame.** A positive, new narrative can quiet negative self-talk. Know your three **Power Assets** that make up your **Power Portfolio** and distinguish between **Truth** and **Tales**.

- **Big talk.** Risk being noticed by speaking up. Do so clearly and confidently. If an important truth might make people uncomfortable, speak it anyway. Stand behind your opinions and beliefs.

- **Cheer every win.** If you don't champion your efforts, who will? Celebrate progress to spur more progress. Write a fifteen-minute email to your boss every Monday with last week's accomplishments and this week's priorities.

- **Don't be a robot.** Self-promote tastefully and pay attention to how your efforts are received.

- **Own your mistakes.** Acknowledge and rectify your shortcomings as transparently as you cheer your wins.

If you're gaining value from this book, I'd be honored if you wrote a review on Amazon, Google, or Goodreads. Instructions at **wildcouragebook.com/review**. You can help others discover their own Wild Courage. (Me asking you to do this? Completely **SHAMELESS!**)

4

OBSESSED

Push, perform, and persist

Obsessed

(adj.): preoccupied with or haunted by some idea, interest, etc.

Obsessed redefined: The courage to set your own standard.

You know you really want what you're going after when you find yourself **OBSESSED** with getting it. At least a little. When doing the work feels important and gratifying, it's a sign you're chasing the right thing. Doing any less than your best feels bad because it threatens to slow your momentum toward that meaningful objective. If you feel yourself lighting up at the smallest sign of progress, you've found something that matters. As a **Trait**, **OBSESSED** helps you tune in to the goals that will feed your soul while simultaneously improving your performance in pursuit of those goals. Being **OBSESSED** certainly put me on the path I've taken toward personal and professional fulfillment.

In 2006, Google was in the news. This was not for its fast and accurate search functionality—people already googled everything—but for its fabulous employee perks. As the war for tech talent warmed up, Google brought the fire: Top pay. World-class benefits. And, notably, a slew of quirky extras to keep its brainy and ambitious employees happy and productive. On-site haircuts, nap rooms, deeply discounted deep-tissue massages . . . the list went on. So did the menu of free food, from burgers and pizza to made-to-order omelets and miso-glazed black cod.

Having just returned from a stint traveling through South America, I needed a job. But as much as I *needed* one, a "job" wasn't what I *wanted*. At twenty-six, I still felt unprepared for real life, whatever that was. Assisting in research efforts at Harvard Business School had been difficult, but it had also felt familiar, like an extension of college. Juggling small part-time gigs when I lived in Israel for a year had been relatively chill. Through the dreamy haze of postcollege freedom, the conventional image of a genuine Day Job inspired genuine dread. Would I really spend the rest of my life getting up at dawn to commute to a dreary glass office building on some highway and fill out spreadsheets? The still-mysterious working world bored me and terrified me at once.

This is why all the breathless news segments and magazine articles about Google grabbed my attention. At the time, a sense of the superlative hovered over the California-based search giant. From a young age, I'd gravitated toward the toughest, the highest, or the best. Why? Competition is exciting. Excellence is inspiring. Now that Google was the *best* place to work and the *most* difficult place to get hired, I wanted in.

A quick Google search—naturally—revealed a handful of open positions at the company's new offices in Denver. So I eagerly applied. During breaks in the process of updating my résumé, I wandered the house exclaiming, "I'm going to work for Google," in a nutty singsong.

This is what it's like to be **OBSESSED**. Think back to when you last felt that kind of inner drive. Every time it happens, it's a clue to what motivates you. Seize it!

Pushing past self-doubt, I submitted the application. Then I waited. And waited some more. Within hours, I was nervous. Within days, I was in a full-blown panic. By the end of the week, I was *devastated*. Why hadn't the recruiter gotten back to me yet? Was it possible—*gasp*—that I'd mistyped my email address?

Anxiously, I scoured my application for the smallest mistake, discovering, to my *horror*, that the upload process had done something funky to the résumé formatting I'd worked so hard to perfect. The blood drained from my face as all my hopes for the future evaporated: "Working at Google was a fun idea while it lasted," I sighed, giving up on my dreams of a better tomorrow. "I wonder if Dairy Queen employees get free ice cream . . ."

Once the initial shock faded, I realized that the Best Company to Work For (and those free massages) still had a hold over me. My inner compass still pointed toward Google. When you're fixated on getting something that doesn't come easily, you can become a puddle of despair and soak into the carpet. Or you can get **OBSESSED** to tap into hidden reserves of energy and ingenuity.

It occurred to me that this formatting problem might also be an opportunity. (It took more life experience to realize that *every* problem can be an opportunity.) My mistake had given me a valid, if paper-thin, excuse to visit the office in person. What did I have to lose? My dignity, sure, but any self-doubt I felt paled next to my unyielding desire to *get that job*. When you're **OBSESSED**, you find the discipline to get out of your own way.

Climbing into my mom's ten-year-old Honda stick shift with a hard copy of my properly formatted résumé, I drove to the address I'd found on Google's recently launched Maps product. At the time, the Colorado headquarters amounted to a couple dozen employees squeezed into a nondescript shared office space.

"Hi, I'm Jenny," I chirped to the building receptionist, brandishing my printout. "I need to speak with someone at Google because there was a problem with my application."

"You can drop it here," she replied. "It's not protocol for them to speak with you."

Protocol, huh?

If you've spent a day of your life seeking work, you're familiar with the silly procedures and policies that organizations use not to select the right candidates but to filter out the wrong ones. Formatting a résumé, spelling everything correctly, and filling out a complicated and buggy online form don't prove your suitability for a role. However, by requiring more care and effort than a (surprisingly high) percentage of applicants are able or willing to supply, these kinds of requirements thin the herd for big companies. Why make the application process easier when you're fielding tens of thousands of résumés a week or more? An arbitrarily complicated submission process is a painless way to weed out unpromising candidates.

This means your first objective in any serious job search is to evade the filters. What good is a fancy degree if no one knows you earned it because you screwed up the submission form?

The fine art of penetrating filters transcends careers and corporations. Life is full of rules serving no function beyond *deterring the deterrable*. The only way through is what I like to call **professional persistence**. Think firm but cheerful. Calm but committed. Agreeable—while steadfastly refusing to agree. My capacity for professional persistence kept me pinned to the receptionist's desk even as every cell in my body urged me to slink back to Mom's Honda. Immediate relief from anxiety, self-doubt, and growing embarrassment lay only fifty feet behind me.

"I need to speak with someone," I firmly but cheerfully repeated, adding, "because I need to discuss my résumé." A behavioral study conducted by Ellen Langer and her colleagues at Harvard in 1978 showed that adding a reason to your request boosts the likelihood of a yes, even if the reason doesn't add meaningful information. In the study, library patrons were more likely to let you skip the line for the copy machine if you mentioned that you needed to make copies. Even though everyone waiting for the copy machine "needed" to make copies. Brilliant, right? People defer to "because."

At least, *some* people do. Apparently, this particular receptionist hadn't reviewed Langer's work yet. She gave me *nothing* for my "because." So the seconds ticked by. My grin melted into a grimace. The smile muscles in my cheeks started to quiver. The urge to shift my weight from one foot to the other became overpowering. Still, I held firm.

Finally, sensing the steadfastness of my professional persistence, the receptionist reluctantly picked up the phone. Moments later, a Googler named Elizabeth met me at the front desk. After explaining the "problem" with my original application, I nimbly mentioned my recent research work at Harvard Business School. For good measure, I added that I'd just returned from working abroad. (I'd heard that working in other countries is a very "Googley" thing to do.) Before I could overstay my welcome, I thanked Elizabeth and waved goodbye as though handing in my résumé had been my only intention.

Feeling lighter than air, I returned to the car and hit the road. Victory!

Or not. Halfway home, I realized I hadn't asked Elizabeth for her business card. What if the recruiter called the house to offer the job before I arrived? My thoughts raced faster than the Honda: "If Mom writes down the recruiter's phone number incorrectly, I'll have to do this again tomorrow!" As it turned out, however, neither Elizabeth nor the recruiter called that day. Or the following one.

When one door closes, the **OBSESSED** kick in a basement window.

Writing down every permutation of Elizabeth's first and last name and respective initials, I emailed all the possible accounts for her at google.com. Doing this felt absurd, but so did my quest to work at a company I knew very little about doing a job I barely understood. What's wrong with a little absurdity in pursuit of what you want? Sometimes, that's what it takes. Don't let your sense of propriety stand in the way of your dreams. Others won't. When they catch what you were too embarrassed to chase, you'll regret it.

Elizabeth wrote me back twenty-three minutes after I sent the last of these Hail Mary emails. Then, and only then, did the recruiter call to set up an interview.

Pursuing something that really matters to you unlocks a well of energy and determination that lesser goals never will. You need this un-bridled fuel to achieve at the highest levels of anything. If you lack the motivation to truly excel, question whether you're pursuing a goal you want or just one you feel you should. Trust your intuition here. The trials of medical school will faze you far less if you're genuinely inter-ested in healing the human body. The trials of entrepreneurship will be much more manageable if you're actually excited to build that business.

To tap into energy, joy, and limitless courage, go after the objective whose inherent difficulties represent an exciting challenge, not a dread-ful burden. If you lack motivation to put the work in, you probably don't want what you're working toward enough. So what will you chase in-stead?

IN DEFENSE OF OBSESSION

As with every other **Trait**, the word *obsessed* carries negative connota-tions. It suggests anything from a nerdish preoccupation with a specific television show or wild-eyed conspiracy theory all the way to dangerous behaviors like stalking and harassment. As usual, this means we're working with a potent concept that's worth reclaiming. Let's harness its sizzling semantic power and use it to bolster us through difficult times.

Obsess comes from the Latin word meaning to set yourself against something, to *besiege* it. Obsession is wading in to fight instead of wait-ing your turn. Rather than let the idea of Google intimidate me into setting my sights lower, I let the size of the challenge inspire me to be-siege that city until it fell.

Obsession derives from two convictions: (1) that what you want mat-ters *and* (2) that you can achieve what you want with sufficient effort. The opposite of **OBSESSED** isn't apathetic; it's fatalistic. If you sometimes feel like your fate is largely out of your control, you know the feeling.

Fatalism is an understandable reaction to a world facing issues beyond the ability of any individual to fix, including climate change, war, inequality, humanitarian tragedies, economic headwinds, and more. However, letting yourself believe you don't have plenty of agency in life is just silly. Regardless of how bad things are out in the world, they'd be *so much worse* if not for the **OBSESSED** people with the courage and determination to set themselves against the seemingly inevitable. Huge, intractable problems get fixed when people get **OBSESSED** with fixing them.

It's easy to ignore all the times things pan out for us thanks to hard work and determination. It's even easier to let a failure or two discourage us. Most of the time, success doesn't come down to luck. It comes down to caring enough to do the job properly. Every day. Whether you're in the mood or not. When you're **OBSESSED**, you show up.

Resign if you like. Quit quietly if you can get away with it. But if you decide to commit your time to something, whether your day job or a side hustle, push yourself to the limits of your potential. Work *should* be a workout. The only way to get stronger at the gym is to do more reps or choose a heavier dumbbell. Sticking with the same effort every time won't build your muscles. Push hard against your limits and expect the occasional failure. If you succeed too easily, you weren't reaching far enough.

High performers overprepare, sweat the details, and go the extra mile. Their colleagues might scoff. Back in school, bullies taunted the teacher's pet. But who cares? Being **OBSESSED** is about achieving your potential *on your terms*, leaving nothing—ambition, talent, or interest—on the table. It means rehearsing your presentations until they're as smooth as butter, preparing a list of priority items before meetings, and using clear and concise bullets instead of long, meandering paragraphs when communicating with VIPs.

Excellence is inspiring. So-so is so boring. And excellence isn't complicated, either:

- Be consistent.

- Be proactive.

- Do one thing at a time—and do it properly.

These bullets might seem obvious, but common sense isn't common practice. It's easy to convince yourself that doing less than you can is acceptable. To get what you want, lose that self-defeating mindset and *take yourself seriously*. Today and every day. If you aren't willing to bet on your potential, why should anyone else?

At a recent visit, my dentist did my cleaning personally. Afterward, he explained that hiring dental hygienists had become difficult. Being **NOSY**—more on that in the next chapter—I asked, "Do you mind doing cleanings yourself?"

"No, actually," he replied. "It keeps me connected to my patients. Plus, I find it satisfying."

His words struck me. Between his extensive training and decades of experience, my dentist is overqualified to scrape plaque for hours a day. He can make far more money with his time doing root canals and bridges than chiseling away at tartar. However, he enjoys the technical challenge of cleaning teeth and the satisfaction of knowing that he's preventing problems down the road for his patients. It's the basic pleasure of a job well done. Even though he's not maximizing his earning potential, he's giving his all to a task that matters to him. Doing this isn't draining, because meticulous effort toward a meaningful goal provides its own fuel. The more of yourself you put into your work, the more you'll have left when the work is complete.

"Craftsmanship means dwelling on a task for a long time and going deeply into it because you want to get it right," Matthew B. Crawford writes in *Shop Class as Soulcraft*. Crawford argues for the psychological and spiritual importance of skilled labor, for *making* things. We undervalue these benefits. Craftsmanship, according to Crawford, "entails learning to do one thing really well, while the ideal of the new economy is to be able to learn new things, celebrating potential rather than achievement."

It's easy to convince yourself that effort doesn't matter if you're able to coast. However, while you might fool your boss, you can't fool yourself. You will never grow and evolve without pushing yourself to do the hard, careful, and deliberate work that tests the limits of your capabilities.

Tomorrow morning, select a task from your to-do list. It can be as simple as handwriting the name cards for a team event. Or as intimidating as drafting a three-page document that lists everything your team should start, stop, or continue next quarter. Target a milestone you can reach in an hour or two. Then, do that one task properly. Prioritize quality over efficiency. To ensure you aren't disturbed while you're working, turn off notifications on your phone and wear earplugs or noise-canceling headphones. Whatever it takes, give this task your complete attention. Don't put it down or switch to something else until you've reached that milestone.

When you're done, sit back and feel your feelings for a minute.

What's going on inside? Chances are, you're experiencing a sense of fulfillment. A small glow of satisfaction. A measure of relief, however tiny.

Don't rush to the next thing. *Notice*. I've grown to love the buzz I get from really conquering a task. I seek that sense of accomplishment in everything I do. That inner surge tells me I'm showing up for myself instead of jumping to what's urgent and letting the world dictate how I use my time and energy.

THE PENCIL SHARPENER

Making things is the best part of work—*especially* in laptop-bound knowledge work, which can feel so ephemeral to begin with. Nothing drains energy faster than a Slack discussion that diverges, a meeting with no deliverable, or a phone call that leads nowhere. Where's the *artifact*? What exists now that didn't back when we started? Too much talking, too little doing. That's the trap of knowledge work. While making stuff takes work, it *makes* energy. It also tends to make your career.

Managers, clients, and investors love *output*. No matter how abstract the task, find a way to make something tangible that you can share with others. Talking about your ideas won't secure funding, close a deal, or get you promoted. Creating stuff with your ideas will. So get something down in writing. When faced with an intimidating challenge like a complex project in an unfamiliar area, do a **pencil sharpener**: create a planning document that you can share with key stakeholders. Do this within twenty-four hours for best results.

For instance, a boss told me five people would be joining my team as part of a larger reorganization. These five employees—four individual contributors and a manager—had skills, backgrounds, and responsibilities that didn't align with the rest of my team. Though the move made sense to somebody higher up the chain with different priorities, it made little sense to me. Oh well. My job was to make it work. To integrate them without disrupting the smoothly running operation I'd worked so hard to build. However, though I understood the objective, I could feel myself intimidated by the idea of getting started. Where to even begin?

When a task gives me a nasty adrenaline spike, I remind myself to start writing. **OBSESSED** redirects anxiety toward productive actions, which alleviate that anxiety. Rather than simmer in decision paralysis, I reached for my keyboard. Bringing five new team members from a different part of the organization into my own would involve research, analysis, and execution.

First, I wrote down the questions I needed to answer: How were these employees currently evaluated? Would I need to incorporate their metrics into ours? Would I need to shift some individual contributors to the incoming manager to balance the load? One manager on my team already had nine individual contributors to deal with . . .

Even though you can do this in a digital format, I call this a **pencil sharpener** because the process works best when performed in a relaxed and informal manner. You're roughing out a quick sketch, not chiseling a master plan in marble. As I got my initial thoughts down in a document rapidly and without much revision, five categories quickly emerged: culture, metrics, manager alignment, change management, and communications. I created headers for each area. Questions, ideas, and next actions accrued under each one.

The next day, I brought a succinct, organized planning document to a one-on-one with my manager. The project was just beginning, but the artifact I'd created in a couple of hours represented a great first step, moving the ball down the field and giving my manager a clear sense of progress.

Why is this technique so powerful for fighting procrastination *and* so delightful to managers? When presented with an intimidating task, a low performer will take a week to "think" (i.e., procrastinate). Rather than risk making the wrong move, they'll stall, putting off the inevitable. When time runs short, they'll panic and return to their manager empty-handed, requesting "more information" or the opportunity to "brainstorm" together.

When managers encounter this behavior, they can't help but ask themselves the same question: What's the point in delegating to someone if I need to coax them to start and hold their hand to get them to finish? It shouldn't take a week to realize you had a follow-up question.

This little dance isn't about missing information but an unwillingness to face the discomfort of uncertainty. You aren't sure of the "perfect" way to proceed, so you just *don't*. The only antidote is **OBSESSED** action. A quick **pencil sharpener**, something as simple as a one-page sketch for moving forward, breaks the anxiety logjam by giving you a low-stakes way to get familiar with an unfamiliar problem. By giving you the opportunity to think through milestones and metrics, a **pencil sharpener** builds confidence, clarifies thinking, and surfaces potential collaborators and other resources. Each step gets progressively easier from there. And for your manager, a written document demonstrates proactivity. It gives them something to react to, a starting point.

Again, do a **pencil sharpener** within a day of receiving any intimidating task. Don't let it sit in your inbox, draining your energy. It'll never be easier to start working on something scary than right after it's been handed to you. Get your thoughts down while the challenge is fresh in your mind—and in the minds of key stakeholders. Because you're creating an artifact early, there are no pent-up expectations to meet yet. People will be less judgmental, more open-minded, and more willing to help when you come to them for answers. If you get out of the gate quickly, you're far more likely to exceed expectations. Something small but real moves the conversation forward, validates assumptions, and gets everyone on the same page. It also builds trust. Trust is essential, especially if you're new and untested.

Your manager says, "I'd like you to find corporate synergy between our footwear and aviation divisions." Huh? Sneakers and planes? Where do I even begin? Let's do a **pencil sharpener**:

- **Goal:** Create project plan to develop flying-shoe product.

- **Self-imposed deadline:** Launch by Q4.

- **Stakeholders:** Emma in footwear, Anton in aviation.

- **Resources:** Assemble team of two or three people with bandwidth and interest (Alex? Sara?) and schedule six weekly planning meetings starting next Tuesday.

- **Assumptions:** We're doing this because of market interest in wearable technology. We can tap into existing in-house expertise in podiatric aerodynamics.

- **Questions:** Do these assumptions sound right? Who else should I reach out to now? What initial output are you looking for? Slides? P&L? By when? How does the above plan sound so far?

Even if your manager disagrees with your assumptions and next steps, you've demonstrated an **OBSESSED**-level degree of care, thoughtfulness, and commitment. Now they can contribute their help without the cognitive effort of starting from scratch. Remember, seniority doesn't come with a crystal ball. If your manager had all the answers, they wouldn't need you. Even if you're out of your depth, add value by giving them a somewhere to begin.

If you do have some idea how to proceed right away, don't hand back a fixed plan. Instead, offer three options, give a clear point of view on each, and make the argument for the one you'd choose. People are more likely to go your way if you've looked at the problem from multiple angles.

Let's say that your manager asked you to help figure out which color bracelets the company should sell next year. Give three options:

- Option 1. Sell red bracelets only.

- Option 2: Sell blue bracelets only.

- Option 3: Sell both red and blue bracelets.

- Recommendation: Sell red bracelets only because X.

By offering three options, you show your capacity to took at things from multiple angles. By offering a strong point of view (i.e., recommendation), you demonstrate the confidence to lead and make tough decisions. By pitching original solutions, you're showing that you're **OBSESSED** enough to take risks that might move the business forward. Managers know how intimidating it can feel to put new ideas out there.

To elevate a **pencil sharpener, double your numbers**. Concrete metrics bring life to any business document. Make a habit of going through each **pencil sharpener** before you share it, and double the amount of numbers or stats you included. If you mentioned three, aim for six instead. Five? Ten.

The numbers you include in your **pencil sharpener** don't have to be fancy, like year-over-year revenue growth projections. You can talk about hours potentially saved, emails that must be sent, or number of meetings involved. In the example above, "Schedule six weekly planning meetings" is stronger than "Schedule planning meetings."

Doubling your numbers feels awkward at first. Don't worry about whether this abundance of detail looks like overkill. Who cares? You're **OBSESSED**, right? Just write as you normally would, count up every fact you've included, and then add that many more stats and metrics. You'll be surprised how much more convincing and effective your writing will get.

Just as a quick and informal **pencil sharpener** gets an overwhelming project off the ground, it's also useful in bringing one in for a landing. When you've completed a complex project, jot down what you've accomplished in a running log. This is an update you can share with key stakeholders who may need reminding of what you've been doing. What's more, you'll be grateful at your next performance review or when revising your résumé—everything you need will be ready. Finally, an accomplishment log boosts morale when your emotional reserves are running low.

Don't forget to **double your numbers** in those documents, too:

Vague: "Had a significant impact on sales revenue."

Specific: "Grew sales revenue $600K (12 percent year over year) despite industry headwinds by launching weekly office hours for customers, which had never been done."

Vague: "Got positive fly-fishing reviews from customers."

Specific: "Got a 9.2 out of 10 rating from fifteen responses about fly-fishing trips I led. Customers specifically noted my friendliness, fish knowledge, and technical skills."

Vague: "Improved test scores."

Specific: "Raised our third-grade statewide math test scores from 72 percent passing to 78 percent passing despite budget cuts by making up songs for multiplication tables."

You did the work. Prove it, above all, to yourself.

FRESH MEET

How often is excellence a solo endeavor? Most of the time, we must enlist other people to work with us to achieve a shared ambition. Sometimes, influencing and motivating people to pursue an objective they don't have much interest in can be frustrating and demoralizing. (See **MANIPULATIVE** for more on that.) This is especially true when you're not operating from a position of authority. Because collaboration often happens in and through meetings, a fresh approach to getting those done properly promises to accelerate all your group efforts.

Karthick Sivanadian is an operations leader at a company that develops medical devices. Unlike his friends in tech who work with software, Sivanadian does work that involves physical devices that save lives. One of Sivanadian's major professional frustrations was scheduling the large meetings required to launch new projects. Simply getting key stakeholders to attend presented a logistical headache. Despite his best efforts, as many as half the invitees—executives, board members, and representatives of partner organizations—would skip these crucial meetings without explanation, creating a huge project bottleneck.

Keeping the meetings themselves on track also proved difficult for Sivanadian. With only an hour to launch a project, attendees would waste valuable time asking derailing questions or going off on tangents. As a result, the decisions required to move forward would get bumped to follow-up meetings, sending Sivanadian back to scheduling hell.

"What brought the most change," Sivanadian told me, "was your advice about sending a meeting agenda to every attendee twenty-four hours in advance. I'd allot five minutes for background context, twenty minutes for covering the problem at hand, twenty for discussion, and ten for deciding on next actions." Creating and sending this agenda before the meeting takes time, but it's a solid investment. "Now, when the meeting gets sidetracked, I can say, 'Hey, we've gone past our allocated time, so why don't we take this offline?'" Even though plenty of attendees are higher up in the org, they accept redirection because the agenda supports it.

Being **OBSESSED** pays off. Sending an agenda in advance keeps meetings on track and also increases attendance and response rates. People who would ignore generic meeting invites respond to detailed agendas, even if they can't attend: "This topic looks great. I wish I could attend, but because I can't, I'll send a designee on my behalf." Sivanadian's approach to coordinating these major meetings, which happen once or twice a quarter, has become a blueprint for all the engineers in his org when scheduling meetings of every size.

A complementary tactic allows Sivanadian to reduce the total number of meetings, making his life much easier: "When I'm invited to a meeting," he told me, "I ask, 'What are you expecting from me?' Half the time, it's crickets. In that case, I simply don't attend. This habit has also propagated to the rest of the team." Thanks to the widespread implementation of these two techniques, meetings have become much more efficient across the board.

Sending an agenda ahead of a meeting seems like simple advice, and it is. Yet, during my corporate career, I received meeting agendas roughly only 10 percent of the time. Even then, I mostly received them from high-level leaders with admins to do the work. That makes sending an agenda a *power* move for a more junior employee. If only bosses send agendas, sending one demonstrates leadership potential.

When you're **OBSESSED**, you don't fling your work at people quickly in the hopes that they accept it and move on. You seek and encourage feedback because you want to improve. When you send an agenda, ask invitees to weigh in. Make sure to include any slides or other meeting-related assets. *Have I left anything out? Did I get the order of the slides right, or should something important be moved to the top so we're sure to cover it?* This will improve the final product while positively influencing the recipients. Nice bonus, right?

Psychological research explains why this step steers decision-making. In 2011, professors Michael I. Norton, Daniel Mochon, and Dan Ariely shared a working paper describing what they dubbed the IKEA effect. They found that consumers place a higher value on things they helped build. In an experiment, participants bid 63 percent more for an IKEA box when they had assembled it themselves. They liked the box more, too.

When we welcome meeting attendees' participation by sharing details about an upcoming meeting and asking for feedback, we make them more invested in the meeting's outcome. They become more likely to attend, contribute, and agree on a course of action.

Send an agenda for every important meeting, from large, quarterly product-planning meetings like the ones Sivanadian plans, to high-stakes meetings with your boss's boss. (You don't need to put in this effort for a casual monthly catch-up with your teammate.) You'll never regret the effort, because you get the time back and more in the form of fewer meetings. Prep tends to double the effectiveness of the meeting itself. To lock in the benefits, send every attendee a short follow-up document summarizing decisions, next steps, and open questions within twenty-four hours. (The most important meeting you'll have each week is likely the one with your boss. You can download a one-on-one template with section headers that increases your impact in that meeting at **wildcouragebook.com/resources**. It can also serve as your agenda. Furthermore, you can download a career development template for biannual conversations with your boss.)

SET YOUR OWN BAR

When Tina Fey joined the writing staff of *Saturday Night Live*, the norm was to start writing on Tuesday night. Fey deliberately set her own bar as a newcomer, starting work alone on Mondays. Why put it off when you have only six days to deliver for a live audience of millions? **OBSESSED** with doing the best job *she* could, not simply fitting in—"I was a nerd," Fey ruefully admits—she became the show's first female head writer and, later, a household name. Few who wrote for *SNL* over the years can match Tina Fey's achievements in comedy.

Growing up, we calibrate our efforts according to the local standard, but why? Your high school friends were probably average. Setting your bar by average will deliver average results, regardless of your true potential. What good is beating your two best friends on this math test or that history project? To get into Stanford, you must stand above top applicants worldwide, not your inner circle. As Tina Fey understood, set your own bar to achieve the extraordinary.

Don't confuse being a good colleague or a trustworthy friend with limiting yourself to the ambitions of those around you. The luck of the draw shouldn't determine how hard you work, how much you learn, or how good you get. When you're **OBSESSED**, what matters is where *you* want to go and how good *you* have to be to get there. **Set your own bar** by identifying concrete performance standards based on your ambitions. Decide for yourself:

- How many hours a week will I spend preparing the grant application?

- How many résumés will I send each week until I'm hired?

- How often will I reach out to the ten most important people in my professional network each year?

No one will ever come and tell you how hard to work to get everything you want. You must figure that out for yourself. Work backward from your goals: If you want to learn basic Mandarin phrases before a trip to China in six months, set a realistic study pace that will get you there. If you discover that you've set the bar too high in one area and don't have the time and energy to meet your expectations, adjust. A rigorous but realistic bar should motivate you to do your best, not discourage you from trying in the first place.

"Easy for you to say, Jenny!" you might be thinking. "My life is hard enough without setting a higher standard." If you're stuck in a lousy job, working for an undermining manager, trapped in a dead-end career, or puttering away passionlessly on a passion project, the idea of setting your own bar may feel impossible. You're not going to *feel* like going the extra mile at first. Not until you see some results.

It's a chicken-and-egg dilemma: (1) You will never be **OBSESSED** about excelling in a dead-end job. (2) Nothing will get you to a better place faster than becoming **OBSESSED**.

Make excellence a mechanical process. Take thinking out of the equation and make what you do consistent and repeatable. Deliberating over how hard to work and for how long only saps mental energy you could use to do the thing. Get your plan down in advance. If you can't muster enthusiasm for your work, automate enthusiastic behavior. Something as simple as the timer on your phone can dramatically improve results by providing structure and motivation. Can you commit to working on your résumé for three sessions of twenty-five minutes?

Or going for a fifteen-minute walk around the neighborhood every afternoon?

When was the last time you felt completely confident that you'd prepared sufficiently for a presentation? If the answer is "never," you're not alone. Few of us rehearse, even for important presentations with career-changing potential. And when I say "rehearse," I don't mean whispering the words to yourself at your desk. I mean standing up and delivering your entire presentation from beginning to end, loud and clear. Stand in a stairwell if you can't find a quiet spot. Use your phone to record yourself presenting, review that recording, and note what you see and hear. Then rinse and repeat six more times. Set your bar at seven run-throughs.

The importance of a rehearsal standard applies to more than just conference room presentations. Whenever you're going to be on the spot and under pressure, seven run-throughs will improve your performance and *reduce your anxiety*. Rehearsal prepares you. Once you know the presentation cold, it frees cognitive capacity to focus on your audience: how they react, agree, and show concern. This mechanical approach to prep will also hone your instincts about how much prep is sufficient for you. You may find you need fewer—or more—run-throughs. Start with seven and judge by your results.

Email is another area in need of a bar raiser. In the past, I'd write endless paragraphs in important emails to stakeholders. I knew I needed to level up at concise communication (see **BRUTAL**), but writing a million emails hadn't helped. I needed to set a new bar. So I made concision a game: I could only use three bullets in important emails. This made writing them more difficult, but because it was a game I was playing with myself, it became something I did habitually. Eventually, structure and brevity came more easily. (For specific guidance on making emails more succinct and persuasive, go to **wildcouragebook.com/resources**.)

To complement numerical standards, use checklists to make a habit of setting your own bar. Checklists are commonplace in high-stakes professions like surgery. As surgeon and author Atul Gawande explains in

The Checklist Manifesto, to ensure the highest level of performance every time surgeons enter the operating room, they follow a step-by-step plan. The checklist gets followed even if they've performed the same procedure a thousand times.

As a trained pilot, I also rely on checklists, consulting them at every stage of a journey and saying each step aloud to ensure I don't miss one: "Mixture rich, avionics on, flaps up . . ." When I take them flying, my kids think I'm strange—"What are you even *talking* about, Mommy?"— but the checklist makes mastery a method, guaranteeing the critical yet easy-to-overlook tasks that ensure a safe flight. If checklists work for pilots and surgeons, why wouldn't one help you excel *consistently*, regardless of motivation level? Your morning checklist might be as simple as the following:

- Meditate for five minutes.

- Exercise for thirty minutes.

- Spend an hour on your most important project before checking your emails.

Does this sound like your typical morning? If it doesn't, what might yesterday have looked like if you followed this checklist instead of your usual routine? Judging from people I've coached, this probably involves responding reactively to every ping while doomscrolling social media in a futile attempt to stave off the stress and anxiety of avoiding the day's most important task.

Give a checklist and timer a try and if it doesn't work for any reason, modify the routine and try it again the next day. Maybe thirty minutes of exercise was a little too ambitious. Start with five and revisit after you've been doing it consistently for four weeks. A checklist is a recipe for spending your time wisely. Refine that recipe based on the results you get.

Don't second-guess any of these methods until you've tried them a few times. If taking your efforts seriously is new for you, your instincts about the effort involved in doing a quality job can't be trusted. If you don't feel committed yet, make it mechanical. **Trust a method over your mind.** Once you see results, adapt that method as needed to optimize the return on your investment of time and energy.

In *Mindset*, psychologist and motivation expert Carol Dweck makes the case for a "growth mindset," the self-fulfilling belief that, with effort, you can improve. Ask yourself: Do you believe that, if you applied yourself steadily, you could get better—not best in the world, but *better*—at anything? Or do you assume successful people are all born with their talent? Dweck's research shows that people with a growth mindset achieve superior life and career outcomes. If you don't already possess one, *yet* is the growth-mindset mantra:

- I'm not a great salesperson *yet*.

- My start-up isn't knocking it out of the park *yet*.

- I haven't met the life partner I'm seeking *yet*.

When I started managing managers at Google, I was new to the team, region, and products. Everyone who reported to me knew more than I did. (*"Impostor!"* screamed my brain.) *Yet* empowered me. "I'm not the leader I need to be *yet*," I told myself. *Yet* got me where I wanted to go. With effort, I got better.

TRAIT TRAPS

Is the juice worth the squeeze?

Once you learn how to build systems that amplify performance, it's tempting to let your efforts run amok. Dopamine and serotonin are powerful drugs! Learning to harness motivation can improve your life, but you must establish guardrails around work to protect your well-being.

Before an important public presentation, I worked with a top communications coach. Even though I was already comfortable in front of a crowd, I wanted to do even better this time. She was amazing, offering tons of useful feedback and advice. Instead of absorbing a few bits and pieces of her vast expertise, I tried to drink from the fire hose and master it all before this one event. For me, it was no longer about getting better. It was about doing the job *perfectly*. If I didn't incorporate everything she told me right away, I'd be a failure.

I ended up preparing for thirty hours, neglecting my day-to-day work in the process. The imbalance didn't register—I was in the groove, determined to adopt fifteen different cues: vary my pitch, optimize my hand gestures, increase pregnant pauses, sound excited but not *too* excited, and on and on. It was too much.

Though the speech itself is a blur in my memory, I remember walking off the stage. Despite the applause, I didn't feel very good: raw, worn out, depleted. Like I'd strained something in my head. As I was driving home that day, it dawned on me how hard I'd squeezed myself for juice that was, in the end, not *that* important. By the time I got home, I was in a serious funk.

"I bombed," I told my husband. No, the audience feedback had been great. Even my highly discerning coach applauded the recording of the event. Inside, however, I felt like a failure. I *had* failed. Managing my mental and emotional health is part of my job. I'd neglected that task and become too obsessed. No coincidence, in my mind, that I came down with a bad cold the next day.

Psychologist Barry Schwartz distinguishes between "maximizers" and "satisficers." Maximizers pursue the best possible outcomes, heedless of the time and effort involved. Satisficers prioritize balance. When they invest in a task, they look for the best return on that investment.

According to Schwartz's research, maximizers get slightly better results but expend *much* more time and energy to achieve them. Despite this, they're less happy with the outcome.

If we're going to make excellence a habit, we must also keep an eye on our psychological safeguards.

Live by limits and leeway

When dealing with an open-ended task or a "launch" of something new, from developing a skill to preparing for a dream vacation, decide how much time and effort to invest *before* you begin (and push it too far). Sketch out a possible cadence and test it out before you commit. Otherwise, you risk vanishing down the rabbit hole—or burning out and losing interest.

For example, you've decided to learn the piano. Ambition is highest at the start, which is why people overcommit with new hobbies and fitness regimens and then lose steam and quit. So set **limits**. Instead of beginning with an idealized practice schedule of an hour after work—only to quit after a couple of missed sessions when life gets in the way—start at a pace that is both doable and flexible: "I will practice fifteen minutes before leaving for work three times a week: Monday, Wednesday, and Thursday."

Plan in hand, stick to that limited cadence for at least three weeks to see how it works out. Is your enthusiasm for the piano flagging by the third week, or do you look forward to each practice session? Are you experiencing any resentment at spending time on the instrument when you could be sleeping in or scrolling through social media? Don't tweak anything until you've vetted your approach under real-world conditions.

Likewise, if you want to build a website for your new consulting business, decide how much time, money, and effort to invest *based on what that website will do for your business*. Do a little research—how complicated are your competitors' sites? For many consultants, a simple page is more than enough to start, and if you're getting a small consultancy off the ground, reaching out to leads and winning new business should take the lion's share of your attention, not deciding on fonts for a landing page. Can you stick to working on the site for a two-hour block each week until it's functional? From there, use web analytics to decide how much more effort is warranted. Guard your time for what matters most.

Being **OBSESSED** is all about consistency. Doing the good thing regularly instead of the great thing now and then. Through experimentation, settle on the investment of time and effort appropriate to the needs of the task *and* be mindful of your other obligations, including rest and self-care. Then give yourself permission for the umpteenth time that day to do things less than perfectly.

If people are counting on your output, break the people-pleasing habit of overpromising. Give yourself **leeway**. We've learned to say yes to the big and no to the small. Even for the big things, however, it's tempting to agree to an unrealistic plan when someone else wants it done yesterday. Before you commit to any goal—internal or external—set realistic limits based on concrete planning. Then, once you feel confident that your plan is reasonable, *pad your budget and timeline another 20 percent* before sharing the estimate with your manager, investor, partner, or child.

If you think you can finish the project in five days, tell the boss they'll have it in six. If you're confident the kitchen remodel will cost fifty thousand dollars, budget sixty. Believe me, you'll be glad you have that leeway when the time comes.

Put life on the books

We like to blame others for our packed calendars, but, as we'll see in **BRUTAL**, this is usually because we refuse to set boundaries around our time. Why is it we're comfortable skipping an unimportant meeting or postponing a call to go to a doctor's appointment or pick up a sick child from school, but not to get to the gym or take a much-needed break? Exercise and rest are crucial to physical health and even more important to cognitive performance. Your manager wants you to prioritize those things, too, but they're not going to manage your time for you. It's your responsibility to put your life on the books.

Every Sunday, before your week fills up with meetings and calls, carve out calendar slots for meals, exercise, rest, social engagements, and play. If you expect world-class performance from yourself, treat yourself like a star athlete. Nourish your body, spirit, and mind, even if that means a quick walk in the park or a trip to the coffee shop to read a good book. You'll hit a wall if you don't schedule time to meet your needs.

If your week is already full by the time Sunday rolls around, consider which thirty-minute meetings you could change to fifteen. Or put these "life on the books" commitments down as repeating events, and review your calendar on a monthly basis to ensure you're prioritizing physical and mental health no matter how chaotic work becomes.

———

Just as with the amount of prep required, you can't trust your instincts about overwork and burnout. Establish guardrails around your efforts *before* you've damaged yourself. With practice, you'll get better at budgeting your energy and prioritizing self-care, but no one is born with these skills. Again, make it mechanical.

Now, brace yourself if the talk about boundaries in the last section left you squirming. If you want to learn what you need to get ahead, you must stick your nose where it doesn't belong. Let's get **NOSY**.

OBSESSED
Push, perform, and persist

- **The pencil sharpener.** Beat procrastination and improve impact by starting every project with a written plan of attack within twenty-four hours.

- **Fresh meet.** Send an agenda to attendees before every important meeting; the IKEA effect tells us that if they are involved in pre-meeting details, you'll get better in-meeting outcomes.

- **Set your own bar.** Establish personal standards that stand apart from the crowd. Use checklists and timers for your most critical tasks and adopt a growth mindset with the word, "yet." *yet.*

- **Is the juice worth the squeeze?** No professional effort is worth depleting your physical or mental reserves. Don't proceed unless you're confident it deserves the bandwidth—and that you have the bandwidth to spare.

- **Live by limits and leeway.** Plan an approach in advance that protects your time and energy on big, open-ended projects. Then, add 20 percent to that estimate before sharing it with stakeholders.

- **Put life on the books.** Block out meals, exercise, rest, meetups, and play on your calendar before it fills with work meetings and calls.

NOSY
Get insatiably curious

> **Nosy**
>
> **(adj.):** of prying or inquisitive disposition or quality.
>
> **Nosy redefined:** The courage to dig deeper.

C uriosity may be dangerous for cats, but it saved my grandmother's life.

Hungary, 1944. Violet—Bubby to me—and thirty other desperate, terrified Jews hid in a cramped apartment while Hungarian soldiers of the ruling Arrow Cross Party swept the streets of Budapest, rounding up candidates for Auschwitz. Tens of thousands of Hungarian Jews had already been sent to the notorious concentration camp, most of whom became part of the six million Jews and eleven million human beings in total murdered by the Nazis during the Holocaust.

When supplies in the hideout ran dangerously low, Violet boldly ventured out for a bucket of water for her fellow Jews. Unfortunately, a group of Arrow Cross soldiers caught her, along with several others, and marched the captives several blocks at gunpoint.

Backs against a wall, the Jews waited to discover their fate: a one-way trip to Auschwitz—or summary execution. The latter seemed more likely; they had already passed several bodies during their short march. Bubby wasn't resigned to this fate, however. My grandmother had always been self-assured and curious and saw no reason to restrain her nosiness now. Turning to face the young soldier pointing his rifle at her, she noticed how tightly he gripped the stock. She summoned the courage to dig deeper and ask a question.

"Excuse me, sir," she said. "What would happen if I stepped out of line?"

The soldier laughed before answering with a Hungarian idiom: "A kisasszony tényleg ilyen hülye, vagy csak tetteti?" In English, "Is the young lady really this stupid, or is she only pretending to be?"

Telling this story in her Florida apartment more than half a century later, at ease in her beloved beige recliner, my bubby clarified that she never intended to disrespect the soldier. She was curious, not just for what he might say but also to judge his mood from his tone and facial expression.

"If he'd cocked the gun and shouted, 'I'll shoot you!' that would have meant one thing," she explained. "But there was a lightness to this young soldier's answer. It gave me a flicker of hope. Staying meant certain death, one way or the other. The way he answered my question left an alternative open."

With a smile and a shrug, Violet left the line without a look back. Heart pounding, she walked down the swastika-lined Budapest street. A moment passed, the heels of her sensible taupe leather shoes clicking on the cobblestones. She tried to breathe evenly. Displaying even a hint of panic would be disastrous. Still, nothing happened. She walked a little faster, yet there was no shout, no sound of heavy military boots thudding into the ground behind her. (All her life, the sound of hiking boots gave Bubby a jolt—she said they make a similar sound.) Eventually, Violet made it all the way back to her refuge, where she waited out the remainder of the war and survived the Holocaust. Most of our family did not.

Am I suggesting that any of the eleven million murdered people had the power to save themselves as Bubby did? Absolutely not. But l'dor v'dor—one generation teaching the next—is an important concept in Judaism. Bubby shared this lesson with me for a reason. Her curiosity saved her life and made my dad's life—and mine—possible. Yes, asking the soldier a question represented a risk, but a relatively small one. The Jews on that street were doomed. Charging at him wouldn't have gotten my slim, twenty-four-year-old grandmother out of that scrape. Nor would threats, bargaining, or promises. Being **NOSY** disarmed the soldier in a way no other tactic could, opening the door to survival. Lucky for me, Violet dared to ask a question.

What questions do you hesitate to ask? Why?

IN DEFENSE OF STICKING YOUR NOSE WHERE IT DOESN'T BELONG

If I had to point to one skill that's gotten me where I am today, it's curiosity. And curiosity *is* a skill. It's genuinely hard for many of us, but *anyone* can work to cultivate it. Lucky for me, curiosity has always come naturally. I'm a busybody, and I'm not ashamed to admit it. Whenever we check in to a hotel, my husband, Jon, steps back from the front desk and gestures at me with an air of resignation: "Go on, Jenny, ask your questions."

Curiosity is an attitude, but it's also a super-practical business and life asset in the right here, right now sense. Want to meet someone special? Tell everyone in your network that you're single. Get on all the apps. Go on lots (and lots) of dates with an attitude of flexibility, openness, and *curiosity*: attention and intention without a rush to judgment. Be **NOSY**, and you'll find your match. It's not magic but simple probability. Maximize those odds by getting curious instead of cynical. As my mom always said, turn worry into wonder. The same logic applies to job opportunities. And investments. And finding that one-in-a-million real estate agent, auto mechanic, or coach. Curiosity opens the faucet of serendipity.

We're born curious. Children under five ask up to one hundred eighty questions a day! However, we're urged to suppress that curiosity as we grow: "Get your nose out of other people's business!" While I don't have a good research-backed figure for adults, I recently observed an hour-long meeting with nine attendees. Six questions total—quite a drop from that childhood figure. This chapter is about reawakening your natural curiosity about everyone and everything. It's powerful stuff, drowning out fear and pulling you toward whatever most aligns with your strengths and values.

Being **NOSY** also draws other people in. Politeness, in the conventional sense, usually means invisibility. (Speaking of which, any cultural emphasis on who should be polite and under what circumstances tells you who's expected to be invisible in that culture.) As we saw in **WEIRD**, **SELFISH**, and **SHAMELESS**, getting what you want requires being seen . . . at the risk of being seen as a little rude. To be noticed, get **NOSY**.

We're all natural journalists. Cultivating curiosity can be as simple as reaching out to people in other departments and asking them about their problems. The answers you hear might clue you in to opportunities for valuable cross-departmental collaborations. If not, you might at least make some new connections at the organization, always a good thing.

Great leaders? They ask *tons* of questions. Conversely, people who ask questions exhibit leadership potential from the bottom rung up. Questions show engagement. They tell the other person that you value their opinion and like to make informed decisions. Put this kid in charge!

Beyond, you know, *answers*—which can be pretty useful in life—curiosity offers intrinsic benefits. Researchers at UC Davis used MRIs to study the effect of curiosity on the brain. They found that putting the brain in a curious state (by asking participants trivia questions for the purpose of the experiment) substantially enhanced learning and memory, *even for facts unrelated to the trivia.* In other words, getting curious about one thing helps you soak up *everything* more effectively. When we're curious, we're open, calm, and receptive. An ideal state of mind for learning and growth.

Bubby's boundless curiosity wasn't all that unusual in her family or among her people. Historically, Jews were locked out of most jobs. Also, they found themselves fleeing town in a hurry based on the local ruler's changing whims. To survive over the millennia, they turned to study: of religious texts like the Torah but also portable skills like metalsmithing, tailoring, and the crafting of jewelry. This is one reason education plays such an enormous role in Jewish culture. We hold curiosity in the highest regard because knowledge can save us even when everything we own gets taken away.

My husband and I started saving for our future kids' college educations on our wedding day. A good education is nothing more than structured nosiness: reading books and asking professors questions because you're too curious to do otherwise. Also, it involves debating meaning and interpretation—the Jews love to debate, whether in a classroom or at the Passover table. The old saying goes, if you ask two rabbis something, you get three opinions. This may be why the Jewish people, who represent 0.2 percent of the world's population, account for over 20 percent of Nobel Prize winners. Nothing can explain that but cultural curiosity. Want 100x results like this? There's no need to convert. Just get **NOSY**.

Ask the CEO how they got where they are. Ask your coworker what they like most about their job. Ask your new manager about opportunities to shadow someone more experienced. Questions are so powerful. After peppering him with questions about his business model and clients, I asked a potential strategic partner whether our consulting services overlapped significantly. Asking this felt like a major overstep. He ran a large consultancy. Would he think I wanted to horn in on his business? My mouth got chalky. The hair on the back of my neck stood up. But I was curious, and to my surprise, he revealed the overlap amounted to 10 percent at most. Partnering with his company led to tens of thousands of dollars in referrals, all because I overstepped. Step up!

Yeah, it's **WEIRD** and **SHAMELESS** to stick your nose where it might not "belong," but we've covered those **Traits** already. While you might feel uncomfortable or occasionally rub someone the wrong way, you'll learn and grow like never before. The questions we burn to ask are essential clues in figuring out what we want before we even know we want it. Let curiosity be your compass.

SPIN THE SPOTLIGHT

Meeting people is simple, but it can *feel* difficult when we're stuck inside our heads, worried about how we are perceived. This makes us self-conscious and awkward. Then others sense that awkwardness, increasing the challenge of connection.

NOSY solves this. Instead of dwelling on whether our shirt is untucked, we observe the other person. Who are they? What do they want? Whenever you feel apprehensive about meeting someone—on a date, in a job interview, or at a work event—turn your perspective outward and draw confidence from curiosity. Networking becomes easier, more enjoyable, and more productive if you approach it as a learning opportunity rather than a directive to "make connections." Sorting everyone you meet into "opportunities" or "wastes of time" keeps you small and scared. Forget what you can get from others and get curious.

"We are interested in others when they are interested in us." The Syrian poet Publilius Syrus wrote this more than two thousand years ago. Dale Carnegie quoted Syrus almost a century ago. Here we are today, still worrying there's something in our nose when we should be sticking it in other people's business.

Socially awkward, introverted people—like yours truly on many occasions—get in our heads about this. Rather than push through anxious feelings, we tell ourselves there is something inauthentic, greedy, or even unethical about connecting with people who might be able to help us or make our lives bigger. Logically, this is silly. People help others for self-serving reasons, even if one of those reasons is a warm feeling of altruism. But altruism is rarely the whole story. If someone gives you a job, you fill a role for them. If someone invests in your business, you give them an investment opportunity. If someone buys from you, you help them address a need. If someone asks you on a date, they get a date with someone special: you.

The logic is clear but doesn't always help with the feelings. Even if we tell ourselves intellectually that every connection delivers value both ways, it can still seem impure, leaving us feeling awkward and self-conscious about something as simple as starting a conversation during a break at an industry conference. Nobody wants to be *that person* (e.g., the waiter who cluelessly shoves his original screenplay at a famous actor along with the bill).

Leading with **NOSY** sidesteps these defense mechanisms. By taking your attention off what you want to get and putting it on the other person's interests, ideas, and experiences, you take the pressure off yourself and restore authenticity to the interaction. The fact that someone can help you in your career becomes secondary to your genuine desire to know more.

Bonus points: Supercharge a new connection by doing your homework. When you know you will meet a new person, learn everything you can about them by asking mutual acquaintances for a briefing or, if that isn't possible, doing a Google search. Again, this is something that feels strange for no logical reason. Why would someone put their work history on LinkedIn if they wanted it kept secret? Same for anything they post on social media—why put it out there if not for *you* to see it? Don't dole out what you've learned creepily—"You sure looked like you were enjoying yourself at the beach on Saturday!" Just point out a shared interest or common experience: "You play guitar? Me too! Do you prefer Fender or Gibson?" The better your prep, the more relaxed and confident you'll be.

There is nothing selfish or manipulative—in their negative senses—here. You're doing the other person a favor by getting up to speed on them. US presidents get briefed before every meeting because it helps avoid awkward missteps. If only we all had in-house research teams to prevent the occasional faux pas. Being **NOSY** helps you contribute more effectively and connect more deeply.

When I was five, my mom took me to the bookstore. We went there often, so the owner, Linda, knew us.

"Ricki, you didn't tell me you were expecting!"

"I'm not," Mom replied with friendly bluntness. "I'm just getting fat!"

Nobody wants to be Linda in that moment, face beet red and mouth agape. Gaffes like this one are usually avoidable if you do your homework first. Get **NOSY** and seek information early, even if it's just a quick, three-minute internet search. (My mom approved this story and says the encounter successfully motivated her to lose the extra weight.)

WOO WITH *YOU*

Whether you're writing an email or presenting to a large group, it's easy to focus on what *you* want out of the deal:

- I want them to offer me the job.

- I want to get that next VC round.

- I want a standing ovation . . . so I get a bigger speaking fee next time.

Get **NOSY** and swap perspectives with your audience: the email recipient, the venture capitalist evaluating your business, or the team sitting through your presentation. The other side is giving you their precious time and attention by reading your writing, hearing your pitch, or watching you present. Shouldn't you know *why*? To get to your desired outcome, figure out what the other side's expectations are—and exceed them. For two seconds, stop thinking about what you want from the exchange and direct your attention outward.

We've been focused on our wants and needs since birth, so this isn't a habit you drop without effort. Here's a simple way to start: As you're writing your next email, avoid starting any sentence with the word *I*. It sounds too simple. However, look at the difference this tiny change can make.

First, the default approach:

> Hi Adam,
>
> I loved the gift box you sent!
>
> I had so much fun doing the session for your team because of my passion for career development. I truly enjoy helping people achieve their goals, so thanks for inviting me.
>
> Next time, I'd love to test out a new leadership training I've been working on. That would really help me improve it.
>
> —Jenny

Now, with the **NOSY** version, wooing with *you*:

> Hi Adam,
>
> Thank you so much for the gift box you sent.
>
> Your team was such a great group. You made it seamless to partner.
>
> Thanks again for the opportunity to contribute to your team's goals.

Next time, your team might benefit from a new leadership training that I'm developing. You could test it hot-off-the-presses if that would be valuable.

—Jenny

The first example has five *I*s, and the second has only one. The latter also three *you*s. Isn't it extraordinary how the same sentiment lands with less *I*? When you focus on your recipient, you engage their attention in a new way. They can feel that warmth, and it changes their attitude. Make *them* the hero, and you *both* win.

Doing this isn't hard—it just takes intention and a few minutes of editing. Over time, writing with *I* will feel unnatural. And writing is only one area where you can swap perspectives. Perhaps you feel self-conscious when walking the higher-ups at work through a slide deck. If so, you're probably worrying about how competent you sound, the points you want to make in the time available, and the impression you hope to convey. The more these concerns steal your attention from your audience, the less likely you are to achieve your aims.

To **woo with** *you* when you've got the mic, add a question to your next presentation: "What are your top Q3 priorities?" or "How can we better partner with you?" Just a single question on a slide in a large font. Open-ended questions engage your audience and, if you pay attention to the answers, help you understand what they want. These slides also remind you to pause in your headlong rush to Win the Presentation. They let you breathe, and your listeners absorb your words. The material might be familiar to you, but it's new to them.

BEHOLD THE BRILLIANT BASICS

"Asking questions shows interest," my mentee Rachel Burke once observed. "It lets others talk about themselves or their project. People *love* talking about themselves or their work—it's human nature." Research confirms Rachel's impression: the brain's pleasure center lights up when someone shares their opinion or talks about themself.

Questions are pure magic. A **NOSY** one can improve any social or professional scenario. From a stressful job interview to a department meeting, good questions add energy to the room, demonstrate engagement, and increase likability—all that before we even get the answers!

This begs the question: What makes a good question? The answer, in most cases, is *an honest one.* Unfortunately, we avoid asking questions that might reveal our ignorance (which, if you think about it, misses the point of asking). The most basic question is usually the most brilliant.

As kids, we ask plenty of questions because we don't know anything, and nobody expects us to. By the time we're in middle school, however, we start to tease each other for asking anything that indicates a lack of knowledge about something "obvious"—even if we're clueless.

Once we're gainfully employed, we no longer risk asking. The shame has been internalized. If we don't know what everyone else appears to understand—whether or not they actually do—we keep that to ourselves.

That's why asking a basic question as an adult is the ultimate **NOSY** power move. What is obvious to the person being asked is nearly always opaque to people other than you. If you're wondering something, odds are half the room is puzzled, too. So ask, and even if you feel insecure mid-question, don't bail. Stick the landing, and don't apologize for not knowing something you don't.

Badass leaders do this deliberately, choosing a moment when subordinates are present to ask a basic question without apology or qualification: "What does TPR mean on this slide?" Entry-level employees, suffocating with impostor syndrome, visibly sag with relief that *somebody* dared challenge the latest of the company's nine hundred obscure acronyms. I always admire leaders willing to set a **NOSY** example.

To frame a question, approach the situation as a complete novice. Let go of your assumptions and preconceived notions. In Zen Buddhism, this is shoshin: beginner's mind. Beginner questions—questions a child would ask—pierce right to the heart of the problem. Leaders ask them. Employees who dare ask them are on the path to leadership.

"Why do we sell courses instead of subscriptions?"

"Why does it take four button presses when it used to take only one?"

"Why is there a sudden drop in this revenue line that's always gone up and to the right?"

Don't worry if you aren't lightning fast on your feet. Think up potential questions whenever you feel bored, frustrated, or nervous in a meeting. (Also, I've included a huge trove of **NOSY** questions you can ask your boss, a mentor, a colleague, your boss's boss, or an interviewer at **wildcouragebook.com/resources**.)

Avoid using questions to show off what you already know. For example, instead of grilling someone after a presentation with technical queries designed to highlight your own expertise, lead with humility:

"How can we most support you on this project?"

"What roadblocks can we remove?"

"What have your biggest learnings been so far?"

These are powerhouse questions whose answers will be genuinely valuable to everyone in the room. (They're also handy if you spaced out during the presentation.)

Questions are also solid icebreakers. The next time you find yourself drifting around at a networking event, find someone standing alone and ask them an open question using *what* or *how*, not a closed, yes-or-no question that won't lead anywhere:

"What was your favorite session so far?"

"What led you to the healthcare industry?"

"How do you know the bride or the groom?"

Open questions like these provide rich answers and leave room for the conversation to evolve meaningfully.

Approaching a stranger with **NOSY** questions feels awkward and scary, but put yourself in the other person's shoes. What do you feel when you're alone at an event and someone else initiates a conversation? *Relieved*. So push past that awkward feeling and pop a question or two. You'll be chatting like old friends before you know it.

Rachel told me something else worth highlighting: "I've found that men ask more questions than women do." Rachel herself was no exception to this generalization. She hesitated to ask questions early in her career. Then, she told me, she got some good advice: "A colleague suggested I ask at least one question in every meeting to help become known and remembered," she said. "I started doing that, and it paid off."

This lines up with my experience. Regardless of gender, if you leave the question asking to people who are more comfortable taking up space in a room, you fade into the background. No one will ever give you permission. You have to grant it to yourself.

STEAL YOUR BLUEPRINT

In the last chapter, you learned to **set your own bar**, establishing your own performance standard instead of blending in with the crowd. There's a corollary to that strategy: imitating someone else's approach. When you experience envy because someone else can do something you can't—*yet*—don't retreat. Revel in that discovery: you want that thing! Get **NOSY** about it. Study your rival with intense curiosity. Deconstruct their approach. Then experiment with aspects of their formula that might apply to you. Why stay demoralized by another person's gold medal when you can melt it down and forge your own crown? It's like matching your pace to a faster jogger for that extra oomph.

If someone's work ethic or skill impresses you, ideally, persuade them to serve as your mentor. Mentorship is always the first ask if you aspire to match someone's example. However, mentorship isn't always an option if that person is too senior to give you the time or otherwise too unattainable. In that case, reverse engineer their blueprint through scrutiny.

This isn't about finding an *overall* role model but deconstructing someone's approach to a *specific*, desired capability. Devote an entire notebook to studying the other person's tactics when giving a sales pitch, leading a team meeting, or delivering constructive feedback. Your colleague may be a jerk, but he writes a heck of a succinct email. How? Whatever they do well, observe it, analyze it, and incorporate what you learn. What appears to be a natural attribute—charisma, for example, or persuasiveness—can be deconstructed and adapted.

For example, when Elijah presents to the organization, everyone is rapt. Leo is impressed—and intimidated—by Elijah's effectiveness. Because Elijah is too senior to approach for mentorship, Leo engages in some **NOSY** espionage. Well, observation. Leo notes that Elijah never hems and haws. No *ums*, *uhs*, or *you knows*. Leo records himself delivering presentations and counts his own until the number goes down. Also, Elijah uses techniques to convey empathy: in the Q&A portion, he thanks each questioner by name and acknowledges their feelings before beginning his answer. Leo writes this tip down on an index card and reads it before he presents. Using Elijah's example as his presentation bar, Leo gradually levels up as a speaker without ever speaking to Elijah directly.

Stealing your blueprint is the perfect jealousy cure. Instead of simmering in resentment, use envy as your engine. Later, when Leo notices his colleague Mollie's project management skills, he copies her whole system, from the spreadsheet template she uses to present results to the succinct but action-inducing wording of her follow-up emails.

Get **NOSY** about your colleagues' and competitors' methods. Make it fun. Become a spy. Ferret out the recipe to someone's secret sauce. And remember that this is completely wholesome. *Example* comes from the Latin verb *eximere*, meaning "to take out." When someone sets an example, following it is the highest compliment. Most people let the success of others keep them playing small, as though there were only so much success to go around. There's always more room at the top! Don't waste your energy resenting someone's special qualities and characteristics when you can steal them for yourself.

SHOULD I GET MY . . .

After nearly every keynote, I get the same question: "Should I get my MBA?" Seeking any form of education or training is the ultimate **NOSY** move. It takes genuine humility combined with heartfelt ambition to (a) acknowledge you have more to learn and (b) invest time, money, and energy in closing that gap, especially when you're already gainfully employed.

NOSY complements **OBSESSED** in that both **Traits** involve refusing to settle with the easy or obvious path when you know more is possible. In both cases, you are willing to invest effort in achieving your potential—for learning and accomplishment, respectively—even though you've already met the basic requirements. Bravo if you've toyed with the possibility of another degree or certification.

Of course, that doesn't answer the question of whether you should do it. If you want to learn more about business—or any other subject or skill of interest—you can do it on the job, from books, or via an internet rabbit hole. Yet there is no substitute for dedicated training, whether in the form of an Ivy League graduate degree, an adult education class at the local community college, a coaching course, or an online software certification.

Beyond satisfying your **NOSY** nature, education often offers the most direct route to advancing your career—or changing careers altogether. For example, many companies won't consider someone for upper management if they don't have an MBA. Traditional professions like law and medicine require specific degrees. Many other careers, from engineering to entrepreneurship, call on skills and relationships most easily developed through in-person and online courses and certifications.

I never got my MBA, but my husband got his, so I've had the opportunity to share the experience vicariously. I also spent three years doing research at Harvard Business School. Everyone's path to learning what they need to succeed looks different. The question is, How do you decide what's right for you? When is formal education worth it, and when does it make sense to get **NOSY** and find a shorter path, one that involves less time, money, or effort?

Consider these questions:

- Do you want to change roles or even enter a new industry?

- How strong is your professional network?

- Do many of those in the upper echelons of your company have MBAs or other advanced degrees? Or do relationships and experience matter more?

- Will your company pay for some or all of the course? If not, can you afford it without undue hardship?

Know your reasons for pursuing more education. Growth happens fastest when we establish a clear hypothesis, run an experiment to test that hypothesis, and then use the results of our experiment to improve. Take the plunge if you have a clear, logical why for school that holds up to scrutiny and the risks are moderate. Any mistakes you make will be honest ones and, therefore, valuable lessons.

If, on the other hand, you're considering a degree because your parents expect it of you, or your peers all seem to be doing it, too, *stop*. Don't get that MBA or MFA or any other advanced degree because you aren't sure what you want to do when you grow up. I hate to break it to you, but school won't necessarily tell you who you are or what you want. There are better ways to explore your interests, from side hustles to volunteer work to internships.

If you want the degree but can't afford it, get scrappy. Figure out an alternative. If nine out of ten execs at your company have an MBA, ask number ten how she managed without it. If you want a skill, start with self-study and see how far you can go alone—even as you save every penny toward the degree. If you want to learn, there is always a way.

One final tip: If you do go back to school, remember that, as my husband once reminded me, happy hour is also a class. Networking is always valuable, and if your school or program is selective, the people in your cohort may play a more important role in your future career than any individual lesson you receive. If B-school guarantees the opportunity for one thing, it's a killer long-term network. Don't bury your nose in the textbook.

TRAIT TRAPS

Don't reinvent the wheel

Asking questions is a power move. Don't squander that power by failing to act on the answers you get. Being **NOSY** isn't just about demonstrating curiosity but benefiting from what you learn. *Take careful notes.* Every time you learn something useful, spend time capturing it. Then review your notes regularly. Ideally, find a way to incorporate that knowledge into your approach.

For example, if a mentor forwards you an email they've used for a cold outreach, don't just archive it. Turn it into a reusable template for the future. Future you will *so* appreciate the effort.

I hoard useful information: pithy quotes, compelling stats and other facts, memorable diagrams, Gantt charts used to plan successful projects—anything that might come in handy later when facing a blank slide deck, document, or email.

The more systematic you can be about creating these tools for your future self, the better off you'll be. The benefits compound over time as your collection grows. Also, by sharing back what you learn from others, you demonstrate that their help is being put to good use. Next time, they'll be even more willing to clue you in. If you truly want to thank someone for their advice, let them see you following it.

Read the room

When seeking clues, don't be clueless. Questions can convey curiosity and interest, but when taken too far or pushed too aggressively, they become genuinely obnoxious or disrespectful. (Remember me and my seventh-grade teacher?) *Pay attention to social cues.* Drop it if a given line of questioning isn't leading anywhere useful or generates irritation or annoyance. If it *seems* like they're avoiding the question, *they're avoiding it*—take the hint!

Early in my career, I sent a top exec a list of mentorship questions and didn't hear back. Instead of taking the hint, I kept bumping the email. Needless to say, that exec did not take me under her wing. When you hit a wall with your questions, take a moment to let the energy dissipate and then try another angle. Or call it a day.

Likewise, asking questions requires the willingness to answer them. No one wants to feel interrogated. That means *reciprocity*. Don't spend the whole conversation asking questions while deflecting those that come your way. If you ask another entrepreneur their monthly recurring revenue and they share it with you, reciprocate that transparency by sharing yours with them. Answer questions with the same degree of vulnerability, authenticity, and candor you expect from others.

Often, we're uncomfortable getting **NOSY** with powerful people because we don't want them to suspect an ulterior motive. As though there were something rude or inauthentic about asking for career advice from someone farther down the path.

Ask away. No one got to the top without help. Someone answered their questions on the way up, and they're almost certainly happy to answer yours. Questions fall flat only when delivered without tact, reciprocity, or follow-through.

Ask politely, prioritize the mutual win, and act on what you learn. You will find that questions deepen every relationship. Being **NOSY** is the first step to building lasting influence. But what use is influence if you're not going to be a little **MANIPULATIVE**?

NOSY
Get insatiably curious

- **Spin the spotlight.** Lead with questions as the ultimate icebreaker. Ask *what* and *how* questions over yes-or-no questions for richer answers. Do at least three minutes of internet research on someone before you meet them.

- **Woo with *you*.** Avoid writing sentences that start with *I*.

- **Behold the brilliant basics.** Asking "dumb" questions is both smart and courageous. Be the brave one who asks what the acronym means.

- **Steal your blueprint.** Replace envy with curiosity and learn from the competition. You don't even need to speak to someone if you can observe them in action and learn from their example.

- **Should I get my . . .** Approach additional education strategically. Don't just get that MBA or professional certification because you're bored with your job or unsure of your career goals.

- **Don't reinvent the wheel.** Hoard templates, quotes, statistics, reports, and other relevant info—your future self will thank you. Report back to mentors and helpers to let them know you took their advice.

- **Read the room.** If you're going to ask questions, be willing to answer them. Pay attention to social cues to gauge when you've pushed it too far.

6

MANIPULATIVE
Build influence
through empathy

> **Manipulative**
>
> **(adj.):** intended to control.
>
> **Manipulative redefined:** The courage to influence others.

Having signed with a top literary agent, I decided to connect with successful authors and learn the ropes from them. (And hey, if they didn't want to meet, I could always **steal the blueprint** . . .) At the top of my wish list? Science of People expert Vanessa Van Edwards, bestselling author of *Captivate* and *Cues*. Vanessa's research-driven insights into charisma, influence, and relationships inspired me long before I started Own Your Career. Dynamite speaker, terrific author, and wizard self-promoter . . . whatever Vanessa did to get where she was, I would do it, too.

Through my professional network, I found a mutual friend to introduce us over email. This happened a few days before work travel would bring me to her neck of the woods in Austin. It seemed like kismet.

I emailed Vanessa: "Though we were just introduced, any chance we could meet this Thursday? I happen to be in town then through

Sunday! I'd love to buy you coffee and hear your thoughts about the book business."

"I can't believe the timing," she wrote back, "but I'm out of town on the same days for a speaking event. Too bad!" Taking Vanessa's friendly refusal at face value would have been easy to do and easier to justify in my own mind. My wish list even included other authors living in Austin. However, I was determined to meet Vanessa herself. Relationships are high-effort *and* high-reward investments. You can't let minor obstacles deflect you.

"Since we're flying on the same day," I replied, "I might be able to swing by your gate to say hi." Vanessa told me that her flight departed at 3:20 p.m. I scanned the departures out of Denver that day and changed my flight to an earlier one.

"What luck!" I wrote back. "My flight gets in just before one." A sixty-dollar change fee to meet Vanessa Van Edwards in person would be a bargain at twice the price. Serendipity isn't found, it's made, remember?

Vanessa and I hit it off. Within minutes, I was drowning in helpful guidance and support for the book you're currently reading. We talked until the very minute Vanessa boarded her plane out of Austin. Leaving the gate, I heaved a sigh of satisfaction. As Harry Potter would say, "Mischief managed."

You may cringe at the **MANIPULATIVE** way I handled this situation. If the idea of using a harmless lie to connect more effectively with someone makes you uncomfortable, you may have limiting beliefs about how and why people connect. We'll dig into those. Also, for what it's worth, I fessed up about the flight change once Vanessa and I got to know each other better. A seeker of influence herself, she found it hilarious.

IN DEFENSE OF MANIPULATION

"Why'd you lie, Jenny? Don't you know your pants are now on fire?" My reasoning was simple. Telling Vanessa I'd change my flight to meet would have put pressure on her, creating tension in a fragile new relationship. She might have felt obligated. For example, if Vanessa's flight ran into an unexpected delay, she might worry about canceling our meeting, considering the hassle I'd gone through. Why create unnecessary stress? I wanted her to feel *good* about the meeting.

While I didn't mind the sixty bucks and wouldn't sweat the loss if the meeting didn't happen, *telling* Vanessa I didn't mind wouldn't lighten the sense of social obligation. We're wired to care about social niceties. When you're in a situation like this, spare the other person the gory details and make connecting *effortless* for them. Sustaining relationships is all about reducing friction. *Make it easy, make it fun, make it last.*

Influence itself is neither bad nor good. How someone *uses* influence is a separate question. That's why I'm leaning into the uncomfortable word *manipulative* here. *Manipulation*, from the Latin root meaning "hand," was coined in chemistry to refer to the physical aspects of the work: pouring beakers of chemicals together, for example. Later, "manipulation" of people took on insidious connotations. *Hey, I'm not a beaker—stop handling me!*

MANIPULATIVE *sounds* terrible, but why? You're damn right we want to manipulate people. Getting people to do things is the only way anything gets done! Does refusing to influence remove influence from the equation? No. It just leaves more room for the unscrupulous few to run the show.

People become uncomfortable examining the mechanics of relationships too closely. We prefer to connect organically, and we sense something icky about approaching others with a strategy. Unfortunately, letting that stop you will dramatically limit the power of your network. To connect with many different people successfully and sustain those relationships over time, squash your squeamishness and muster the courage to seek out and use your influence. Without a strategy here, you're leaving the health and longevity of all your relationships to chance. Those few born gorgeous and magnetically charismatic who happen to live and work in the coolest neighborhood of a major city will still be fine. The rest of us will need to be **MANIPULATIVE**.

Everyone is happy to build relationships that promise mutual benefit, but few like seeing the sausage get made. So network deliberately, but don't let others see you sweat. There was no benefit to Vanessa's knowing about my flight change fee. That would be weird, not **WEIRD**.

MANIPULATIVE is the most counterintuitive **Trait** because nearly everyone trusts relationships, even their most important ones—spouse, kids, parents, business partner—to sort themselves out without conscious effort. Over and over, we take our relationships for granted. Then we wonder why we have only two close friends in middle age, both from way back in college. Or why our trusted cofounder wants to be bought out of the business. Or why our spouse picked up and left us "all of a sudden." "But I thought we were doing fine," the surprised divorcée tells everyone.

If you've ever had a close relationship fail for reasons you didn't understand, ask yourself whether you invested regular effort in maintaining that relationship. Relationships are living, breathing things. Invest time, effort, and thought in them, or they will crumble.

A new relationship is where you need to invest the most care and attention. Recent connections are very delicate. When you first meet someone, their immediate reaction is positive or negative based on superficial details like what you're wearing or how you carry yourself. If you want to be judged on what matters—integrity, intelligence, talent, experience, humor, *whatever*—it's *your* job to prove those attributes using strategies like the ones in this chapter. Never expect the other person to put the work in to figure out whether you're worth knowing. They won't.

Why are some people so utterly convincing and credible? So effective at motivating and leading others? Charisma appears in community organizers and cult leaders; it isn't tied to the message but to the messenger. Some make friends wherever they go. Some people persuade others so easily they should require a license. Why? And why do others have the opposite effect, lowering the energy in every room and sending minglers fleeing for the drinks table?

Equally important to this chapter is another question: Why does skill with people inspire negative emotions? "She's so *manipulative.*" You're saying it's bad that she gets others to do what she wants? I'm curious: What are *you* trying to accomplish when you talk—massage eardrums?

What is intrinsically bad about getting people to do what you want? Call it leadership if you want, but that word is so overused it lacks any potency. Whatever the label, people in any walk of life succeed by befriending, convincing, motivating, empathizing with, and rallying others. Why did you open your mouth if you weren't trying to get someone to do or think something? We manipulate constantly. Then, we call it "catching up," "shooting the breeze," or even "parenting."

With nine minutes left to get the kids to school, you can bet I will employ manipulation tricks to bend my kids to my will. For example, I give Ari his choice of two shirts. This gives him enough agency to feel independent . . . without derailing my agenda. Pretty devious, right?

Real, sustainable influence is built on *mutual* benefit. People who create mutual benefit influence others by communicating the upside of *being* influenced. For example, an accountant convinces you of her reliability and expertise through advertising, marketing, and word of mouth. Watch out: she is manipulating you into hiring her. Next, she manipulates you into trimming your tax bill by 15 percent by changing how you file. Brainwashed, you work with her year after year and recommend her to your friends. Don't you have any self-respect, letting yourself be manipulated like that?

This chapter explains how to create mutually beneficial relationships that elevate your work and life goals instead of putting your energy into the draining, dead-end, default relationships that hold you back.

Being liked *matters*. You will never change the world for the better if you can't warm another person's heart or change their mind. It doesn't matter how good you are at your job if people dislike you. Ultimately, every company is a social group that also needs customers. Business is social, period. Your boss and your boss's boss, among many others, play huge roles in whether you succeed. Likewise, you must find mentors to teach you and sponsors to advocate for you. To achieve your ambitions, these people and many more must like you and want you to succeed. Can you get ahead if a couple don't? Sure, but few factors limit your reach more than the ambivalence, let alone dislike, felt by others around you.

The most effective tools of manipulation are honesty, generosity (of time, effort, and praise), and thoughtfulness. Thank project contributors by name. Send follow-up emails summarizing key points within twenty-four hours of an important meeting. Give people the opportunity to offer feedback on your projects. Then show them that you acted on that feedback. Know your audience and speak to them with *their* values, preferences, and goals in mind. Adapt to your colleagues' working styles. Offer help proactively instead of waiting to be asked.

Shifting focus from your problems to those of others will quickly change how your ideas and suggestions are received. Call this outward focus "empathy" if you want, but remember that empathy isn't about being a doormat. It's about paying attention to others. Trying to understand them and caring about what you learn. What do they like? What do they want? What do they want to avoid? In other words, it's about being **NOSY**. From there, it takes minimal effort to balance their needs and preferences against your own. Often, it means so much to see someone make the slightest effort: cheer a recent win, ask after a sick spouse, or order a vegan option for the brainstorming session.

Revved up to give manipulation a try? Take a moment and jot down your **Dynamic Dozen**: twelve people you'd like to meet over the next twelve months. These might be key figures in your organization, influential voices in your industry, or impressive role models. Get **NOSY**. It's enough for now to set an intention and start thinking about how you might "manipulate" these people into lending their aid. For example, if you haven't yet connected directly with your boss's boss, get **MANIPULATIVE** and include them. It may feel odd to reach out to someone two levels up, but speaking as someone who spent years as a senior leader, I can confirm that the benefit goes both ways. You're closer to the action. That's a valuable perspective.

If you're currently hunting for jobs, amp this up: aim to interview twelve people in twelve weeks. Leverage your network and make it happen.

PLAY POLITICS

At a speaking event, I asked an audience of two thousand people, "What frustrates you the most about your career?" The dominant answer was, as you might have guessed, politics. Office politics are a significant professional headwind for most of us. I navigated Google's rapids well enough, but politics kept me up at night more than the milestones, metrics, or deadlines.

Initially, I believed playing politics wasted time and energy that could be used to get work done. However, pretending politics didn't exist, or that playing politics was something better left to the manipulative, made things worse. Politics become a *bigger* headache when we don't talk about them openly. They become much easier to manage once you accept they exist and discuss them with others transparently.

Look at it this way: If power is the electricity that drives an organization, politics are the circuits along which power flows. What we call "playing politics" boils down to managing relationships . . . with clear eyes about how people operate. Politics can be managed ethically or otherwise, but all work relationships must be handled with human nature firmly in mind.

It's *your* responsibility to figure out the flow of power in your organization. Who makes the decisions, and who steers the decisions made by those people? Usually, these latter individuals sit at the intersection of different departments, using their position between, for example, sales and marketing, as leverage for getting things done. Once you understand who pulls the strings, get **MANIPULATIVE**: find these string pullers and pull *theirs*. Invest your time in connecting with the connectors. Build relationships and create mutual trust and value exchange. Eventually, you will join their ranks. It's time to get over your squeamishness around power:

Talk power. To start playing politics, get past discomfort with the word. Talk about it. Politics aren't a taboo but a tool. A *power* tool. The power you accumulate through politics can be used to achieve important things *and* advance your agenda *without* undermining others or crossing ethical lines (more under **Trait Traps** below).

Navigating politics can be even more challenging for women and other underrepresented groups. That makes talking about it openly even more important.

King's College London researchers interviewed minority employees at large companies across different industries in the United Kingdom. The majority reported negative experiences dealing with office politics, "feeling excluded from informal relationships, being overlooked or pushed aside by managers, and witnessing underhanded behavior from their peers." As a result, these employees had ignored politics altogether, "missing out on vital development opportunities and relationships needed to succeed."

However, in some cases, employees reported cultures "where managers proactively included minority employees in the kinds of political activity necessary to be effective in their jobs and advance in their organizations." Crucially, things got better not by ignoring politics but by adding *transparency*: "Rather than feeling slimy or underhanded, office politics were openly acknowledged and even taught to newcomers." In other words, simply giving new employees the lay of the political landscape—the dos and don'ts, the pet peeves, the animosities and alliances—helps diminish or even erase the negative impact.

"There's no escaping office politics," one of the researchers concluded. "It might get a bad rap, but the ability to network, build relationships, and influence others is critical in any workplace."

As a leader, discuss politics openly. I didn't mince words at Google with my direct and indirect reports: "Don't go to X about this. X will sit on it because he doesn't like Y. Go to Z and get it done." Plain talk, rapid results.

As an individual contributor, roll up your sleeves. The less power you have, the more important it is for you to get **MANIPULATIVE** and seize some. If your manager isn't open about office politics, ask your peers:

- Whose buy-in do I need to fast-track this project?

- Should I consult with X before taking this action or simply update X once it's complete? Whom should I cc, and whom should I bcc?

- What's the best time of year to put in a request for budget?

The answers to these questions and many more are vital to your job at any organization. They fill the unwritten chapters of the company's operations manual. Keep asking people with power until you find one willing to give you a glimpse of that manual.

Map power. "Power, while it eludes definition, is easy enough to recognize by its consequences," according to management professors Gerald R. Salancik and Jeffrey Pfeffer. It's "the ability of those who possess power to bring about the outcomes they desire." To show how easy it is to recognize power, Salancik and Pfeffer asked department managers in a large organization to rank their peers according to influence. There was almost no disagreement on the top five. (The lists differed only in how participants ranked their own influence, naturally enough.) The professors successfully replicated this result at factories, banks, and universities. We know who holds power and who doesn't.

Org charts are hierarchical. *Power* flows in a network pattern. Imagine dotted lines of influence crisscrossing the actual org chart, leaping between departments and across functional silos. These lines represent friendships and other connections that bridge gaps between domestic and international sides of the business, creative and production, sales and marketing, and so on. Mapping these dotted lines will make politics at your company easier to understand.

To map power in your team, department, company, or even industry, take out a piece of paper and put the most powerful person at the center. Next, surround that center name with five of the next most powerful people from your perspective. For each of those names, draw more lines, expanding the web of influence not by function but by relationship. Who spends time with whom? Who can count on whose ear? You can't be **MANIPULATIVE** until you know where to manipulate.

Often, power in a business concentrates where money comes in (e.g., sales), not where value is generated (e.g., product design). Not always, though. If financial success depends on cutting-edge tech in a hot field, in-demand engineers might rule the roost. As a real estate developer, my dad dealt with power up close his entire career, and this was his golden rule: "Whoever has the gold makes the rules."

Mapping power lines will clear up all your work mysteries. For example, when a project stalls for no apparent reason . . . until a certain person returns from vacation and momentum mysteriously returns. Or a seemingly great idea generates vocal, across-the-board support . . . until someone from another department speaks against it, at which point all that support evaporates.

Seek power. Get in the room. To gain more power, you must spend time where it's wielded. If there's a regular business review meeting for top leaders, ask to sit in "to learn more about high-level priorities." Or "to see our other leaders in action." If you work closely with another org within the company, ask to sit in on its leadership meeting: "Hey, sales has a weekly revenue report meeting, don't they? Open to my sitting in once in a while? It would help me understand the needs of your sellers better." In most cases, access is easy for leaders to grant. In the words of Congresswoman Shirley Chisholm, If you don't have a seat at the table, "bring a folding chair."

Power grows through proximity. Get adjacent to it. Rub shoulders with the elite. Listen, pay attention . . . and be seen. For people to know you, they first have to recognize you. So be visible. Be present. Be **MANIPULATIVE**.

FLUENT IN INFLUENCE

Being **MANIPULATIVE** is all about extending your influence, and management is how we exert influence at work. We manage people to influence them. *Management is manipulation*, and being properly **MANIPULATIVE** extends far beyond our direct reports.

Some management resources discuss "managing up" (i.e., investing effort in a productive and healthy relationship with your manager). However, this encourages a two-dimensional view of your work relationships: up or down. Remember those lines of power running like a web throughout the organization? Manage relationships in *every* direction to be *fluent* in how you *influence*. This doesn't mean sending an occasional email or text, either. Connect face-to-face (in person whenever possible) and at least voice to voice. You'll never build and sustain a meaningful connection through text alone. When connecting with someone, go to them. If you can't, pick up the phone. *Fluent in influence* consists of four strategies: manage higher, manage diagonally, manage sideways, and manage outside.

Manage higher. Your boss's boss plays a major role in your career trajectory, but a poll of my followers revealed that nearly 40 percent have never set up time to meet with their skip-level manager. It's time to get **MANIPULATIVE** and manage higher. (If you're already well acquainted with your manager's manager, apply the following to the next rung above them.)

It's normal to balk at going above your manager's head. In an earlier era, this was tantamount to mutiny. The gray-suited businessmen of the 1950s were mainly World War II veterans, soldiers trained to respect the chain of command. Those midcentury office politics have changed. In modern organizations, developing a relationship with your skip-level manager isn't seen as manipulative. It's usually encouraged. That said, alert your manager first, just in case, before sending a note to their manager.

To arrange a meeting, lead with praise. We all have egos. To boost the odds of a yes, make the other person feel good by saying something nice about them.

I point out the obvious here because acknowledging ego is so frowned upon at companies. We all like to pretend we're objective in every decision we make. Nonsense. In reality, we like people who like us, and we help the people we like. You have an ego, and I have an ego. Likewise, your manager and your manager's manager both have egos. Accepting the obvious facts of human nature is key to being **MANIPULATIVE**. So let flattery smooth the way:

I hope you're well! First, I appreciated your recent email to the team. Thanks, in particular, for including all the decision-making details behind the recent reorg. It gave me a better sense of where we're going as an organization. Your transparency was inspiring.

On a related note, you mentioned in the email that [insert project] is a priority for the quarter. I'd love to discuss playing a role. Also, I have some successes from [related project]

I could share. Could I work with your admin to find fifteen minutes to connect?

Once you've got time on the books, get **OBSESSED** and overprepare.

- **Bring data.** Assemble data from recent and current projects so you can tout your clear impact. Also, bring your last deck: walking through the first few slides provides an opportunity to emphasize recent wins *and* demonstrate presentation skills. If you can, pull customer feedback or other frontline data. This adds value for them. It's easy to feel out of touch as a high-level leader.

- **Bring value.** Tell them three of your **Power Assets**: two business skills and one people skill. They may start liking you, but you must show them why they might need you.

- **Bring questions.** Start the meeting by asking specific, grounded questions about their plans and vision for the future of their org. This **NOSY** strategy demonstrates knowledge, curiosity, and ambition while warming the room. (Remember, we *love* being asked questions about ourselves.) Also, the answers can be illuminating.

Feeling some butterflies is normal. I still get nervous before emailing or meeting with powerful people. Remember, you can offer value to your skip-level manager no matter how little experience you have. If you're new to the company, you have a fresh perspective on its hiring and onboarding process (although you'll want to stick to the positive in any first encounter). If you're not new, you can offer a ground-level perspective on active projects that the leader can't easily get elsewhere. To calm your nerves, keep in mind that they're a person, too, and that they have their own boss. Even a CEO reports to a board. We're all human beings who put our pants on one leg at a time.

If your skip-level manager seems receptive, close the meeting on a **MANIPULATIVE** note: Ask for the best career advice they've ever received. Or for one thing you ought to be doing that you aren't doing already. Or for what they wish they'd known about the industry at your stage. Finally, propose the idea of quarterly check-ins moving forward.

The first time you do this feels like a big lift, but the payoff can appear quickly. Your skip-level manager might already have an opportunity in need of the right person. The courage to schedule a meeting like this will separate you from the crowd. (You can download a slide template to use in this meeting at **wildcouragebook.com/resources**.)

Manage diagonally. While pursuing a director-level role at Google, I strategically built relationships with five out of seven of my manager's peers to influence their decision. My promotion wouldn't have happened as quickly if I hadn't been **MANIPULATIVE**. Developing connections with those up and sideways on the org chart matters.

Though it might not be transparent from where you're sitting, your manager isn't the only person steering your future at the company. At medium- and large-size organizations, it's often a committee that decides performance scores and promotions. Your job is to figure out who else sits on that committee and get them to know you. If your manager has five peers, connect with at least two. A friendly voice or two chiming up at the right moment can make all the difference. The last thing you want one of those voices at the table saying is, "Promote *who*?"

(Of course, the idea is to seek significance once you've done something significant. Don't chase a promotion six months into a new gig . . . unless you invented a new antibiotic or signed Beyoncé as a client in those six months.)

Building relationships with your manager's peers feels scary, but the stakes are lower than when reaching out to your skip-level manager. They're not directly above you in the hierarchy, so both sides know it's a long-term play. The idea is to ensure that your assets as an employee are known to more than just your manager.

The **MANIPULATIVE** approach is to offer to collaborate on a cross-departmental project or seek feedback on something that touches their team. Make sure you're offering value. As always, start with *their* needs. Then make the ask in person if feasible, or send an email:

> Hope you're well! [My manager] mentioned that your team is launching something similar to [active project of mine]. I thought your team might find it useful to hear about the setbacks we overcame, and I'd value your feedback on our approach. If you're open, I'd love to schedule a time for us to discuss this.

As with your skip-level manager, **OBSESSED** preparation will determine the effectiveness of this meeting. Bring data, value, and questions. Can you volunteer to mentor a junior member of their team? Or present some juicy internal research to the group? Handled correctly, these people represent your best candidates for future **mentors** and **sponsors**, so spare no effort.

A **mentor** is someone who speaks *to* you. A good one is a source of professional guidance and can offer invaluable transparency into office politics. A **sponsor** is someone who speaks *for* you and *about* you. They're the senior managers who speak in your favor behind the scenes. Mentors *guide* careers, and sponsors *shape* careers. You need both. (I've included scripts to land a mentor or sponsor at **wildcouragebook.com /resources**.)

After the meeting, follow up with a quick thank-you email within twenty-four hours. Send a note every few months to update them on something cool or interesting in your part of the business. Ask about another one-on-one meeting once or twice a year. These notes will cement the positive impression you've built over time.

With mentors and sponsors, it's crucial to act on at least some of their feedback and *tell them that you did*. This shows them you take their help seriously. If you don't take this step, they're unlikely to continue investing time and energy in you. So close the loop: "By the way, I cut that presentation down from twenty-five to ten slides as suggested. See attached. It was a big hit. And, by the way, I loved that podcast episode you recommended. Thanks again!"

Manage sideways. Don't neglect your peers. Nurturing these relationships is common sense, yet so many people make the mistake of seeing those to their left and right as either casual buddies or competitors to be bested. Neither mindset aids your professional growth.

Look at it from a **MANIPULATIVE** perspective: Today, they're your coworkers. Tomorrow, they may occupy senior-level positions at the company. Over time, they will move on to other organizations in your industry, broadening your network and opening the door to new opportunities— or closing doors and poisoning wells, depending on what they remember about you. How will they respond when you reach out down the line?

Maintaining healthy peer-level relationships isn't rocket science. You probably already meet with these people regularly, so consider what might level up the relationship. Share data and information with them generously. Also, give credit liberally. For example, sign emails from both of you when sending something you've collaborated on, even if you did the lion's share. Bump their signal by commenting on threads or in person when they speak up about an idea or project. This kind of behavior strengthens the relationship and builds your influence across the board. Leaders are impressed by the willingness to support peers. Amplifying others is an undeniable leadership trait.

Manage outside. Even if you love your job and have no near-term plans to move, invest regular effort in the **MANIPULATIVE** building of professional relationships outside your organization and even your industry. Your network provides crucial support in advancing your career, often in unexpected ways.

The lowest-hanging fruit here is to stay active on sites like LinkedIn and connect online with people who interest you. You can also attend conferences and other industry events, volunteer for industry-related nonprofits, and join industry-related organizations. These are all excellent ways to get in the room with people who might become useful contacts.

So many people I meet *despise* networking. Unfortunately, this aversion limits our options when changing jobs, shutting us off from serendipitous opportunities. It's easy to say you love your current role and company when you're unaware of better gigs that are available. Most desirable positions are earmarked for certain candidates before the company posts them on job boards. Your odds of being considered are nil if you're not on their radar by the time you see the listing.

To overcome your resistance to networking, adopt a new mindset. Reframe it as managing *outside*. Anyone you meet at a conference or party could be your future manager, direct report, or investor. Think of everyone you meet as a friend you haven't made yet! It's silly, but it works.

Because people are people, the same principles of influence apply. When emailing someone for coffee or a call, lead with praise, offer value, and ask for something specific. Start with a recent social media post or notable professional accomplishment:

> Your recent LinkedIn post on [topic] caught my attention. While I'm happy in my role at [company], I am avidly interested in [topic], and your insights struck a chord. Would you be open to a short call? You might find my recent market analysis interesting, and I'd love to bring your perspective back to my team.

You can trade information from your unique professional vantage points (short of corporate espionage, naturally). Or help them forge new relationships in your organization. Or provide a limited form of your professional service as a free sample.

Finally, look for an opportunity to inject a little **WEIRD** into your **MANIPULATIVE** efforts. For example, when following up, you might send your message via a short audio recording. When a post I share with my followers goes viral, I get hundreds of direct messages and one or two audio messages. While I do my best to read some DMs, I always listen to the audio ones—they stand out. What are some ways you can stand apart?

To grow as a dealmaker, impasse breaker, and all-around mover and shaker, **warm the room with positive energy.** You might be great at solving problems and creating mutual benefit, but people have to like and trust you enough to let you prove it. Logically, being right should be enough, but feelings beat facts. Or, as Teddy Roosevelt allegedly put it, "Nobody cares how much you know until they know how much you care."

Every job is a service job. You buy coffee from the barista who greets you with a smile every morning. How are your clients, customers, collaborators, and coworkers any different? Being **MANIPULATIVE**—influential, persuasive, *heeded*—gets easier when people like you. You can squeeze results out of people with fear, but affection, empathy, admiration, and respect are more powerful and lasting by far.

People gravitate toward you if you add positive energy. Resistance to your ideas, suggestions, and requests melts away with a little personal warmth. Being likable sweetens every deal. So start by being honest with yourself. How often do you warm the room versus cool it down? If meetings with your team are always somber, the morale problem starts with you.

Do you carry negative emotions from one encounter to the next? You don't want the sour vibe from a disappointing performance review to ruin family dinner. That's what happens when we're sloppy about our emotional state. Enter a team meeting in an irritable funk because a client call went south, and it will absolutely undermine your agenda. Instead, try to shift gears. Even a few deep breaths in a quiet room before your next meeting, call, or presentation will make a difference. *Especially* when you're convinced you're too busy to take a few minutes to reset!

People who lead with positive energy aren't always genuinely *feeling* the warmth they're conveying to others. When someone consistently brings warmth to every encounter, that takes work. It's a **MANIPULATIVE** decision. They muster good mojo for others even if they hit traffic on the commute or lost a few hours of sleep to a colicky baby. Being a net-positive energy investor is a strategy, not just a matter of temperament. And while mustering warmth can feel impossible at times, it doesn't require that much real effort: a smile, a little bounce in your step, or talking about a project as glass half-full. Next time you meet with some-one, force yourself to stand tall, make eye contact, move purposefully, and add a friendly greeting. It gets easier with practice.

Finding the right title for this book involved a lot of back-and-forth. A *lot*. Seventy-five options were considered, with plenty of spirited dis-agreement among the stakeholders: my agent and I, of course, along with all the people involved on the publisher's side. This could have been a draining process, but the warmth and positivity my editor, Lydia, brought to the discussion kept it fun and *effective*.

Every time Lydia shared new possibilities, she'd write something like, "Here are six more title ideas. I think number one and number three are particularly great. We are getting *so* close. I'm excited!" This lands so differently than, "Here are six more title ideas to consider." En-ergy is *contagious*. If Lydia was excited, then heck, I might as well be excited, too! Her warmth kept me motivated and engaged throughout the grueling process that culminated in *Wild Courage*.

Warmth isn't complicated. It can be as simple as framing a neutral message in a more positive way. This is less about some magical com-munication skill than consistent effort to add a steady drip of upbeat energy to every situation.

Sometimes, warmth goes only one way. Your manager may arrive scowling to your annual performance review despite your purposefully sunny demeanor. Remember that the other person's mood has nothing to do with you if you just arrived. They probably don't even realize what they're doing with their face and body. Maybe their last meeting ran long, and they're worried about staying on track. Maybe they just re-ceived a troubling email. Maybe they have a sick parent.

Meeting stubborn coolness with more warmth is tough, for example, when dealing with an important but prickly new client. When we don't feel a sense of psychological safety, we assume every scowl is intended for us. Likewise, if we lead with energy that isn't reciprocated, our natural response is to meet fire with fire. Remind yourself that the other person's affect has nothing to do with you. There's no benefit in retaliating. Eyes on the prize.

GENEROSITY RECIPROCITY

It might seem odd to say this in a book about courageously going after what you want, but we get more by giving. Giving to others gives life meaning. It feels good and brings us closer to the people we care about. And it helps us influence others like nothing else. Generosity is an easy and profoundly *underused* tool for getting what you want. If you *take* nothing else from this chapter, *give*, give, and give some more.

My friend Jenny Blake, author of *Free Time* and *Pivot*, sent me a lovely gift box containing a pair of fuzzy pink socks, among other cozy items, as a thank-you for a business favor. I think of her whenever I wear them (like I am as I'm writing this). When I sold my book proposal to a top publisher, I planned to send Jenny a thank-you gift for introducing me to my wonderful literary agent, Lisa. Jenny beat me to it, sending another gift box to congratulate me on the sale. These gifts warm my heart every time I think about them.

Does Jenny's generosity make me feel connected to her and eager to help whenever possible? Absolutely. Knowing someone wants to build a stronger relationship doesn't make the gift less meaningful. Never hesitate to give for fear that the recipient suspects your motive. You know, they know, and nobody cares—we all have motives!

Also, as mentioned earlier we all have egos. We like it when people do things for us, and we like *people* who do things for us. Once you understand the central role of generosity in human connection, you're ready to do as Mo Bunnell suggests and "give to grow," which is also the title of his latest book.

Mo runs Bunnell Idea Group (BIG), an Atlanta-based firm that trains high-level client service professionals like lawyers and consultants in business development. BIG teaches experts how to build stronger relationships with people who will pay for their expertise. Top organizations like Sotheby's entrust Mo with their best employees because of his effect on business growth. With Mo's training, experts attract and retain more clients and do more business with each one.

Mo knows from experience that nothing gets you more of what you want than giving others what they need. Early in his career, after a promotion from a role spent creating complex financial models, Mo found himself responsible for building relationships with senior leaders at major organizations. The first such relationship was with the chief human resources officer of a global financial organization. How would he win over a seasoned executive twenty years older than he was to drive more of her business to his company?

Convinced his future hinged on their first meeting, Mo decided to go for broke, working with peers at his firm to design small but valuable projects his company could lead as complementary "investments in her success." He asked each top colleague to contribute a one-hour topical discussion with the client on their area of expertise, or "phase zero" of a project on the company's dime to build momentum. Having secured internal support, Mo attended the client meeting with his handwritten list of possibilities, hoping at least one or two appealed to her.

"She liked the first one," he recalled, "and she liked the second one, and she liked the third one, nine out of ten, so I was like, 'Wow, this is *working.*'" The client organization got plenty of complementary value from the projects, but that generosity paid off. Each of those giveaways translated into paid work for Mo's company *and* a stronger client relationship. "The best part," Mo recalled, was that coordinating the delivery of these "give to grow" projects helped him develop relationships with the leaders in his organization. This experience became the seed of Mo's company, BIG.

Last year, Mo contacted chief revenue officers and other business development leaders at two dozen BIG clients and asked them to estimate the revenue difference between average and top performers: the consensus was 10x. What made the top performers different? "They offer *more help more often*." Yet Mo and his trainers still encounter generosity skeptics, "people who think you do business development and build influence by not giving anything away until you're hired."

If you give a client *everything* for free, you'll quickly go broke. According to Mo, a "strategic giver" gives without expectation of return but scales the gift to the size of the potential payoff: "If your boss's boss wants five hours of your time, give it to them," Mo said. "If someone who went to the same college cold emails you for an informational interview, do a twenty-minute call and ask them to do something first to gauge their commitment. We don't give our all to everyone who asks."

Avoid these three generosity pitfalls:

1. **Too much.** Don't solve their whole problem. Leave them wanting more. Like a good novelist, close on a cliff-hanger.

2. **Too nice.** Don't pack up your bags and leave after you've been helpful, hoping they'll call you one day. Make a specific recommendation that leads to business: "This was a great start. From here, I recommend hiring us to do the following. . . ."

3. **Wrong audience.** If you're investing in a client, you have the right to request that all decision-makers be in the room to see it.

Mo points to the IKEA effect, first mentioned in **OBSESSED**: people value things more highly when they play a role in creating them: "They need to *weigh* in to *buy* in," he said. "Propose any project or deal as a work in progress, and give them a target of how much to modify: This is about 80 percent right, but you know your organization better, so I need your help to make it great. What would you change?"

Strategic giving is the foundation of Mo's **MANIPULATIVE** business strategy. Even his books, which package up a substantial portion of his corporate training for a minuscule fraction of the cost, represent a "give to grow": "Every two hundred copies sold translates into a hundred-thousand-dollar training contract. Many people read the book and get all they need, but a few say, 'Our whole organization needs this. Can your team fly around the world and teach these concepts to our company?' Helping people creates the opportunity to help more people."

TRAIT TRAPS

Manipulation gone wrong

Sway people, don't shove them. It's easy to become so focused on achieving your objective that you stomp on the other person's sense of agency. Don't be that manager. Don't be that partner. Don't be that person.

Manipulation has a bad rap for a reason. If you get what you want but leave others feeling used or even abused, you're missing the point of this chapter. As Mo Bunnell advises, everything works better when we build solutions together for a mutual win. The idea is to lead people toward an objective that serves everyone. If you're leading and they're not eager to follow, you've misjudged either the objective or their need for it. Stop pushing and start listening and empathizing. Whatever you do, don't force it. You might break something.

The authenticity trap

"Bring your whole self to work" looks great on a poster, but it doesn't bring you any closer to what you want.

"If we hire a professional to do surgery on our knee or paint our house," Seth Godin said, "we don't want them to show up and say, 'I had a fight with my spouse, and I'm going to do a lousy job.' That would be authentic, but not what we want! 'No, please, fake being the best surgeon in the world today because that's what I hired, and that's what I need.'"

If you're at work, stay professional and lead with warmth and positivity, even if it's momentarily *inauthentic*. In most cases, the other person will be receptive to that effort and warm up to you. Ideally, you can drop the act and build a real connection over time. If not, keep your game face on and get the job done.

Don't fawn

Express positivity with everyone you meet, but don't kiss anyone's butt.

Status in a relatively egalitarian country like the United States operates differently than it does in cultures where class is strictly defined and carefully communicated. In some countries, there is no ambiguity about who defers to whom. Not here. The org chart at a company tells you who *reports* to whom. As discussed, that chart rarely lines up with the actual status of each person. Also, we tend to collaborate with others in establishing relative status. We look to each other for clues, which is why acting deferential actually lowers the other person's impression of your status. You're telling them that you're not on their level. That you aren't a force to be reckoned with. They may have been in doubt, but now you've confirmed their suspicion, and they may never take you seriously.

The next time you network with a powerful person, resist the instinct to fawn. Instead, adopt the mindset of an equal partner in a value exchange. Talk like a person: bring up a nonwork topic like the new painting in their office or that crazy storm the day before. Not politics, not religion, just friendly banter. Even better, give *them* an action item. Or a piece of constructive feedback. As power moves go, this is a risky one. However, the willingness to speak your mind conveys authenticity and helps level the field. You might be an intern, but in the eyes of the marketing director whose site you helped improve, you're an intern to be reckoned with.

Giving feedback isn't about personal attacks, of course. Offer something useful and relevant, and make sure you're operating from a position of strength. If you're confident in the advice and its objective merits, go for it.

When I give specific and constructive feedback to people I've just met, it surprises them but almost always takes the relationship from surface to serious. For example, I once volunteered tough feedback to a senior VP. It quickly established my credibility and leadership potential with him, jump-starting a strong connection. Later, that VP invited me to a half-day one-on-one coaching session in California. This person was used to everyone fawning over him, so my risky move elevated me. It almost certainly helped lead to my becoming an executive.

You'll have to be **SHAMELESS**. Telling an industry hotshot what they can do to improve their launch plan or the company CRO that they're a little hard to hear when they're presenting can feel like overstepping. However, people nearly always appreciate useful, well-meaning feedback. The higher the other person's status, the more infrequent honest feedback becomes. Once you hold power in an organization, it can feel like you're in a bubble, with no clear sense of how you're actually doing. You learn to value the truth tellers. That's why taking the risk to speak truth to power establishes your value and helps you stand out.

"This is super helpful," a bestselling author replied to my unsolicited suggestion about his website when we connected. "Can't thank you enough! It's rare to get such candid, helpful feedback. This is gold! Please keep it coming anytime, especially the opportunities for improvement around anything you see me doing. It's great to have a fellow author out there to up my game, and I'd be happy to return in kind." Thank you, wild courage.

Are you feeling a little more comfortable operating with warmth, positivity, connection, and charisma to get what you want? In the next chapter, we address the other side of the coin: being **BRUTAL**. Sticking up for your needs may not make more friends, but it drives away the bad ones.

MANIPULATIVE
Build influence through empathy

- **Play politics.** Instead of pretending office politics don't exist, discuss them with your team and navigate them together. Politics are unwritten chapters of the company's operations manual; figure out whose buy-in you really need to make things happen just as you would figure out how a crucial piece of equipment works.

- **Fluent in influence.** Fearlessly manage relationships in every direction to increase your impact within the organization. To build influence, connect with your skip-level manager, your boss's peers, and anyone who might make a good mentor or sponsor. Consistently add good energy to every email and encounter through word choice, tone, facial expressions, and body language.

- **Generosity reciprocity.** Nothing builds influence like authentic generosity. Give to grow with your time, ideas, and network.

- **Manipulation gone wrong.** Influence, inspire, and motivate—don't use.

- **The authenticity trap.** Be authentic appropriately. You can be yourself and stay professional. Sometimes you have to keep your game face on and still get the job done.

- **Don't fawn.** Stand up for yourself; exhibiting self-worth establishes status. Feel confident going toe to toe with people in positions of power and influence.

7

BRUTAL

Draw lines and stick to them

> **Brutal**
>
> **(adj.):** unpleasantly accurate and incisive.
>
> **Brutal redefined:** The courage to protect your time and energy.

Being **BRUTAL** is about setting lines between what's OK and what's not. Between what you will and won't do. Because good, strong boundaries *prevent* problems, often invisibly, it's easy to discount their importance . . . until you see what happens when you *don't* set them. **BRUTAL** works like an insurance policy that way. You put regular effort into this **Trait** because it works in the background to keep you safe, healthy, and happy.

I learned the importance of **BRUTAL** the hard way when a failure to set boundaries led to one of the most difficult moments of my life. A few years ago, I needed to be in New York City for work. Because my in-laws live on Long Island, I brought Noa, five at the time, for her first solo visit with Mimi and Pa. After handing her off to them at LaGuardia airport, I took a cab into Manhattan for several consecutive days of face-to-face meetings with Google colleagues.

Over breakfast with one of my direct reports the next morning, I saw a missed call and voicemail from Audrey, my mother-in-law. The text transcription appeared: "Please call me." My stomach dropped.

"Noa is OK," Audrey said when she picked up, "but there was an accident." During an M&M cookie-baking session that morning, Noa's hair had gotten caught in the mixer, tearing some free from her scalp. FaceTime revealed a bald spot on Noa's sweet little head. Thankfully, she wasn't bleeding, and Cousin Bob, the pediatrician, had done a video inspection and deemed the injury minor. Noa's hair would grow back. However, her emotional pain was immense. She could barely speak through hysterical tears: "Mommy, please come," she whimpered. "I'm *not* going back to school. Everyone's going to make fun of me. Please, Mommy. Come, *please!*"

Noa's words cut me like a knife. Naturally, a huge part of me wanted to drop everything and comfort her. However, when Audrey asked me how soon they could meet me in Manhattan, I hesitated. The only free slots on my calendar were 12:15 p.m. to 1:00 p.m. and 2:30 p.m. to 2:45 p.m.

The inevitable rationalization kicked in. I told myself Noa would calm down before they left the house. Remembering her other childhood injuries, I figured she would stop crying before we even ended the call. Then, bored to tears in the car for two hours, she would drive Mimi and Pa crazy. My poor in-laws, stressed to near hysteria already, needed a long schlep through traffic with a bored five-year-old like a . . . well, they didn't need it. Also, I worried that Noa would refuse to return to their house after seeing me again. I'd have to manage her for the rest of my trip.

"Rationalization is a weapon so powerful," Dan Pink told me, "it should require a background check." Within ninety seconds, I'd gone from panic mode to anxiety-tinged business as usual.

"Noa will be fine," I told Audrey. "There's no need to bring her all the way into the city. I'll see her in two days at the airport."

I ended the FaceTime and returned to my cooling egg-and-cheese sandwich with a complete lack of appetite. My direct report, a mother herself, suggested I opt out of leading the town hall later that day. *No, too important.* Likewise, I couldn't bail on my subsequent meeting with peers from Google's India headquarters—they'd taken a sixteen-hour flight! Nor could I skip the rare in-person one-on-one with my New York–based manager.

My colleagues could not have been more supportive. My manager told me to do whatever I needed to do to care for my daughter, reassuring me that *"everything* is cancelable." But I couldn't stop thinking about All. Those. Meetings. My executive assistant at Google stacked each weekday like a *Tetris* board: thirty-minute meetings back-to-back with a quick gap for lunch and two short breathers. Keeping each *Tetris* block in place felt vitally important. One move would create a cascade of shifted and missed meetings that might last days, even weeks. The idea of all that hassle . . .

Even as people offered to rearrange their agendas, I continued to rationalize the decision to stick with mine. Checking in throughout the day with my in-laws, I learned that Noa was dancing with her little cousins with her new, pink-sequined baseball cap on. She was *enjoying* herself. That gave me an out, and I took it. At one point, I even told myself that taking Noa for the remainder of the trip wouldn't have been fair to her grandparents. I still harbored guilt about moving the grandkids to Boulder in the first place: "They deserve this time together."

When I finally saw Noa in person two days later, she nervously removed her pink hat, and I gasped. The patch of missing hair was *so much bigger* than I'd let myself believe based on the FaceTime call. The size of a *grapefruit*. My heart sank. What had I been *thinking* by attending meetings instead of caring for my daughter?

Instead of drawing a line and prioritizing what really mattered, I had failed Noa and myself. The truth was that I had failed to muster the courage to make a hard but necessary call no matter the consequences. All I had to do was say no to my work agenda and say yes to my daughter. In other words, draw a boundary. Instead, I failed to meet the standard I'd set for myself.

Boundaries make life easier: healthier, calmer, and more manageable. Having clear boundaries and being **BRUTAL** about enforcing them is the key to getting what you want. While most of the discussion in the book has been around pursuing professional success, what use is any of that if you fail as a person? Being a good mom was and is more important to me than any professional objective. Instead of hopping on the Long Island Rail Road to give my daughter what she needed—a hug from Mommy—I taught her that work mattered more.

For the following two years, I felt a pang whenever I noticed Noa's patch of slowly growing hair. The experience made me seriously question my capacity as a mother and heightened all my already roaring insecurities about how I voted with my calendar. Sure, I *said* family was my number-one value, but did my *actions* support that?

They call these hard calls for a reason. While we can blame others, hard calls are hard even when we have external permission and support. Here, I took the easy path, and I still deeply regret it. It's not easy to be a mother and a career-driven professional. Having our nanny do school pickups was one thing, but this was a moment of truth for me, and I blew it. The failure showed me how vital it is to draw boundaries with others and ourselves about what we need and what is important to us.

While leaving my daughter hanging was brutal in the given sense of the word, the **BRUTAL** call would have been to do what was right instead of what was easy: canceling everything and going to Noa's side. **BRUTAL** is about drawing protective lines with others and around our time and energy to prioritize what matters most.

IN DEFENSE OF BEING A LITTLE BRUTAL

No is a complete sentence. Give it a try when no one's watching: "No."

For both sides, boundaries can feel, yes, **BRUTAL**. When someone asks you on a date and you reply with a flat-out "Thanks, but I'm not interested," people say, "Man, that was *brutal*!" The conventional response is to let them down "easy" instead. The irony! A friendly but firm refusal is much easier on the other person than equivocation. While it may not feel great for a few minutes when you get shut down cold, how much worse is it to imagine romantic potential where it doesn't exist? Nothing is more punishing than the friend zone. Here and elsewhere, "no" is an act of mercy.

We must also draw boundaries with ourselves: our time, our agenda, our priorities. When I asked a mentor how he stayed sane with everything on his plate, he said, "Ruthless prioritization." Every minute you spend doing one thing, you actively say no to everything else you might be doing instead. When you invest money, energy, or mental bandwidth in one pursuit, you deny those resources to the rest. And some of those other activities are also really important!

Multitasking is a lie. You choose . . . or you let the choices be made for you. To achieve your goals, you must *commit* to spending your time and energy in accordance with your true priorities, no matter how painful it sometimes feels. Without learning to be **BRUTAL**, you will never achieve your highest goals, whatever they are. What use is a bucket list with holes in your bucket?

When I say "painful," I mean it. **BRUTAL** hurts. Even telling a total stranger what we want can feel so uncomfortable that we'll do what we don't want to do just to avoid an awkward confrontation. Remember in

SHAMELESS when the waiter served cold potatoes? Send the potatoes back. Always send them back.

According to fMRI research, some of us light up more in the anterior insula region of the brain when forced to disagree with others. This region regulates social emotions and bodily sensations, so heightened activity there suggests that conflict *feels* worse for some of us. If you've always struggled with confrontation, you might be fighting an uphill battle. However, knowing this is an area of growth doesn't let you off the hook from working on it. In fact, it suggests there is even more upside to developing this **Trait** for you. To thrive, you must get more comfortable being direct, clear, and consistent with your words and actions.

Those in power tend to use social conventions to test our boundaries. You'll notice how abstract notions like "tact," "grace," and "duty" are wielded to keep us in line—until we learn to draw lines of our own. The boss expects the employee to cancel holiday plans out of loyalty to the company, but when *the boss's* holiday trip is on the line, the idea of duty goes out the window. Phrases like *team player* and *going the extra mile* are used to paper over leadership problems like understaffing and poor planning. When the "rules" apply only one way—toward *you*—you must set boundaries to protect yourself.

Establishing boundaries with others is tough but necessary when pursuing your goals: "I need weekend mornings to launch my real estate side hustle." You'll need to be **BRUTAL** to get what you want. Whether telling your parents to use your new pronouns or telling your boss you need a new hire to cover your team's added responsibilities, expect a clash of wills.

Again, being **BRUTAL** here doesn't mean being angry or vicious. It means being direct, decisive, and clear about what you need. Think fierce self-centeredness (see **SELFISH**). If you stuff your feelings down instead, the resentment you experience will manifest as petulance, passive-aggressive behavior, "unexplained" anger, depression, burnout. . . .

Like most people, I used to ignore conflict or hide from it. Against all my natural inclinations, however, I developed a threshold for awkward confrontations. Now, I tackle them head on. When a colleague said something in a meeting that rubbed me the wrong way, I left feeling frustrated and hurt. My old pattern would have been to keep my feelings to myself, silently stressing about every encounter with the other person. Instead, I asked him to meet me in a conference room. One awkward, five-minute conversation cleared the air and put us back on good terms for five years and counting. We rationalize avoiding these necessary conversations, creating so much long-term suffering to avoid short-term discomfort!

Logically, finding out why you were passed over for an opportunity makes sense. Even so, most people don't request constructive feedback when they don't get a freelance gig, role, or promotion. "Too awkward." *Ask anyway.* (Get **NOSY**.) The sting to your ego will fade, while the information gained may alter the course of your career. For example, one interviewer told me I needed to develop my executive presence. Instead of arguing the point or getting defensive—"Is that *code* for something?"—I took the feedback at face value and got to work on it. With effort and practice, communicating with top executives became one of my recognized strengths as a leader at Google.

Is it "brutal" to tell a colleague where they can improve at work? No! It's *generous*. Genuinely mean would be telling everyone *else* that your colleague is failing *behind their back*, something far too many of us do because we're unwilling to be direct. Worse, we internally categorize this as kindness. Yes, people will passive-aggressively trash a colleague while basking in their righteousness: "I'm a good person!" they think, "because I'd never say this negative stuff to their face. That would hurt their feelings!"

When you offer a mirror to a colleague in the form of constructive feedback, it's an act of generosity. Cutting the bull and telling someone how to improve is helpful. It's also brave, bold, protective, clear, direct, and authentic. Being **BRUTAL** in this sense is hard to stomach if you're not used to it, but so worth it. Dealing with awkward, unpleasant, and cringeworthy situations is like removing a Band-Aid. The faster you tear it off, the better. Spare your direct report any equivocation during their annual review. When you know a romantic relationship is doomed, tell them "It's over," not "We need to talk because I'm not sure how I'm feeling anymore about this." Life is too short to take anything but the shortest path between two points. When someone is mad because what *you* want doesn't align with what *they* want, don't dilute the message to mollify them. Tear—ouch!—and move on.

What if you're dealing with an underperforming direct report? Here, it's even more important to deliver constructive feedback quickly and help them turn the situation around. Sure, say it tactfully, but say it clearly, too. Then, if they don't improve after being given a fair chance, let them go. Don't sit on it. If you keep the ones who aren't a fit, you lose the ones who are.

A close friend, Kim, backed out of a wedding she'd felt pressured to agree to for religious reasons three days before the event. Obviously, this hurt the groom's feelings. However, would it have been kinder to him (and any future children) to go through with it because it was too late to get a refund from the caterer? Rather than cave to social pressure only to divorce years or months later, Kim made the **BRUTAL** call. Later, she married the love of her life, and they have been happy together for years now.

BRUTAL means drawing lines around what is important, as I failed to do with Noa. Putting the important ahead of the urgent. Trimming emails to their essentials. Delivering short, punchy presentations. Skipping unimportant meetings and unnecessary tasks. Cutting, clarifying, and prioritizing can be terrifying if you've always been more reactive than active. It's time to stop letting the needs of others override your goals. You'll learn that people value your time more when they see you placing value on it first. With practice, **BRUTAL** becomes second nature.

PERMISSION GRANTED

Once you get **BRUTAL**, you grow to *love* the freedom it provides. The energy it releases. *Carpe diem* doesn't go far enough. Value every hour like you value your own life. Time *is* your life! Give yourself a permission slip to defend every *minute*—that minute will never come back. Use each one and make it count. Once you stop frittering time to please others, that sense of being stuck falls away. Progress accelerates in every area of life. However, you must push yourself out of your comfort zone to achieve that growth.

I still experience guilt about not being a good enough parent. (If you do, too, you're probably a good parent. The bad ones aren't worried about it.) Many of my therapy appointments center on "mom guilt" and pushing through that guilt to pursue my own goals and interests, like carving out the time to write this book. Helping people have the courage to go after what they want or advance their careers is *important*, not just for me and those I help but also for my kids. They're proud of me. They're inspired by what I do. In fact, Noa loves to write little books and tells everyone at school that she's an author, just like Mommy. During one party where kids were doing various art projects, she confidently plopped herself at a table to work on a book entitled *The Mustache Pug*. I felt so much pride. I realized that my kids need to see me pursuing challenging and important goals even more than they need me baking cupcakes from scratch to share with the class. (The kids prefer the store-bought ones anyway—I always cut the sugar in the recipe by at least a third.)

That pang of guilt or anxiety—"Am I allowed to *do* this?"—is a good sign that you're setting a new boundary in a healthy spot. That you're acting instead of just reacting. Instead of avoiding pangs of uneasiness, seek them out. Turn **BRUTAL** up until you feel a little flutter, like when you were a little kid and did something "naughty." Instead of imagining what others will think of you when you break with convention, use that inner flutter as your compass when deciding how far and fast to carve your path.

- "Skipping that unnecessary meeting today to finish my deck feels dangerous—*good.*"

- "Ignoring that unsolicited email feels rude—*I can live with that.*"

- "Staying in and completing this task instead of going out for drinks with colleagues makes me feel guilty—*What use is looking like a team player if I let the team down on this deadline?*"

- "Hiking each day at 4:30 p.m. when I could be with my kids feels **SELFISH**—*oh, right, that's good!*"

- You can download a daily tracker—one thing you want to do more of, one thing you want to do less of, at **wildcouragebook .com/resources**.

Heroes don't tire themselves out by fighting every foot soldier on the battlefield. They carve a path to the main villain. If you beat *that* guy, you become a champion. So let's get legendary.

Why does doing the important stuff that matters (instead of responding to every email and attending every meeting) feel So. Damn. Hard?

Early in our careers, we fall into the trap of *performative work*. We don't know what efforts truly matter to business outcomes yet. Or how people manage to climb the corporate ladder. With nothing better to fall back on, we default to being responsive. Jumping on every incoming task, email, and meeting, we flail around thoughtlessly in an attempt to look super busy at all times. When we don't know how to contribute effectively, we invest our energy in convincing others that we're committed to the task and, therefore, useful. Worth keeping around.

In contrast, the true powerhouses blithely stay at their desks when everyone else scurries toward some performative all-staff meeting. Why? They're doing stuff that matters. Call the real stuff *rewardative* work.

Doing rewardative work requires being *unresponsive* at times. Saying no to people. Ignoring minor issues. Closing your email tab. If you want to knock that market analysis report or product launch out of the park, you must spend hours sitting quietly at your laptop instead of running from meeting to meeting.

Performative work is a *painful* habit to break (a) because of the discipline and concentration required by rewardative work and (b) because we imagine everyone's judgment. "What's Jenny doing just *sitting* there? Doesn't she know how . . . *not busy* she looks?" **BRUTAL** is the art of feeling those feelings and doing what matters anyway.

Sharp, clear lines between work and personal make a huge difference, because each area distracts us from fully engaging with the other. We're half-present with our loved ones or when trying to enjoy ourselves. We're half-distracted when our work tasks require focused attention. Once you've separated your work time, draw lines *within* it:

- Do the most important thing first.

- Don't switch tasks until you've reached a significant milestone.

- When someone interrupts you, say, "Sorry, I'm busy now. I'll find you later."

Believe it or not, this simple, three-step process is how every major thing you've ever wished you'd accomplished yourself actually got done by that other person. Without these three steps, I never would have reached a senior leadership position at Google, launched Own Your Career, gotten my pilot's license, or published this book.

Value. Your. Limited. Time.

My aunt Lori and uncle Michael love the theater. However, they don't hesitate to **leave at intermission** if they aren't enjoying the show. They do this despite having paid good money for those seats. While this doesn't happen often, seeing lots of plays ensures that some will be stinkers. For Lori and Michael, cutting their losses makes sense. The money's gone. So is the first hour of their time. Why sacrifice another hour they could spend enjoying cocktails at a nearby bar or strolling around an interesting neighborhood?

In my twenties, I forced myself to finish every book I started, no matter how dull or infuriating. As though each book were a course of antibiotics that I had a duty to complete. Growing older, I finally realized that I would never get to read all the books I would love. Not even the tiniest fraction. If I hoped to read more of the good ones in my lifetime, I'd have to leave at intermission, bailing on books that didn't grab me by the third chapter. Life's too short to finish everything you start. You can use that time and energy in many ways that matter more. If this book is not adding value for you, stop reading it. Right now. Do not read one more sentence.

You just read another sentence.

When something isn't paying off, leave at intermission. Prioritize opportunity cost (the stuff you can still do with your remaining time and energy) over sunk cost (the time and energy you will never get back). Whether it's a dead-end project, a relationship going nowhere, or an irrelevant work meeting, nothing is gained by "seeing this through." Find an excuse and vamoose.

DON'T CRY OVER SPILLED EMAIL

One analysis found that the average worker spends *2.6 hours daily* on email. Email is important, but *within limits*.

Bestselling author Neal Stephenson once confessed to being a genuinely bad email correspondent: "If I organize my life in such a way that I get lots of long, consecutive, uninterrupted time-chunks, I can write novels," he explains. "But as those chunks get separated and fragmented, my productivity as a novelist drops spectacularly. What replaces it? Instead of a novel that will be around for a long time, and that will, with luck, be read by many people, there is a bunch of e-mail messages that I have sent out." Maybe you're not writing a novel, but every email deletes time you might invest in something important and meaningful.

The surefire way to ensnare yourself even further in the email trap is following the misguided advice to "clear" that chaotic inbox. Lunacy! Emails are like rabbits—they *breed*. Send one out, and you're guaranteed to receive one or more responses. The only solution is to get **BRUTAL** and stem the flow for good with the four Fs:

Filter. Use filters to separate newsletters, notifications, and other casual communication from the important stuff that requires a response. You should always respond to emails sent by your boss, clients, *and* direct reports—this is one of your most important jobs as a manager (see **BOSSY**). Beyond that, default to no response unless you find a really compelling reason to do so. (Remember, emails breed!) Likewise, unsubscribe from nonessential mailing lists and mark spam consistently instead of deleting it.

Focus. Tackle email only during certain blocks each day, preferably when your energy is low and you'd be spacing out anyway. The rest of the time, close your email app. If you're tempted to peek, block the app with productivity software. It's hard to resist that little rush of dopamine you get by replying to messages, especially when facing a daunting task requiring concentration. At home, don't charge your phone in your bedroom. That way, you won't go into immediate fight-or-flight mode from an upsetting work email when your eyes are still half-closed. This is *really* hard to do, but challenge yourself to try it for fourteen days. (Yes, this does mean spending ten bucks on an alarm clock.)

Free. Before your next vacation, free yourself of the burden of catching up. Set an away message: "When I return from vacation, I will archive any messages that arrived while I was away. To ensure I read this email, reply with 'please read' in the subject line." Set up a filter to put emails with "please read" in the subject line in a special folder. (I've included useful email scripts for controlling correspondence and setting expectations on response times at **wildcouragebook.com/resources**.) Then, when you return from your trip, archive everything else. Don't even scan the subject lines. Before my last vacation, I estimated that 10 percent of my emails would get the "please read" treatment. Out of nine hundred, only four did. Shows you how important most emails are. Why take a week off only to spend the following one desperately trying to "catch up"?

Feel. Once an email makes it through the filters, take a moment before responding and notice your feelings: *Am I responding only for perception, attention, or emotional relief?* If writing a response feels compulsive, like you *must* send it right away, chances are it isn't necessary. Or that your words might come back to haunt you. Look at your inbox and sort your last ten responses according to your reasons for sending it—function versus feeling:

A) Function: to answer a question that advances a project, leave a paper trail, start a collaboration, delegate a task, address many people at once, or work across time zones.

B) Feeling: to show responsiveness and dedication to my team because I'm anxious they think I'm not paying attention, reply all to a thread without adding anything meaningful, or feel productive by checking something off.

Responding to the occasional email for a B reason is OK, but understand the distinction. Start questioning every feeling-driven response. Before clicking send, ask: Will this move things forward? Or will it just clog someone else's inbox? Will it resolve the issue or exacerbate something that a face-to-face conversation would solve?

Is it worth my time?

The four Fs will do far more to restore inbox sanity than any misguided attempt to dig your way to the bottom of your inbox. Your inbox has no bottom, so there's no use crying over spilled email.

Next, shorten your email. We receive so many emails at work because of the back-and-forth caused by sloppy communication. Because people skim emails, they're far more likely to be confused by overstuffed ones, even if you included everything they need to know somewhere in that mess of paragraphs. So they write back to clarify, and now you're going back and forth trying to straighten up the mess.

Brevity is the soul of **BRUTAL**. While direct, concise emails take an extra moment or two to complete, they are far more likely to do the job in one go. Start by cutting emails by 50 percent. Remove the throat clearing at the start, the muddle in the middle, and the unnecessary digression at the end. Chop that email up like a madman and laugh maniacally while you're doing it. **BRUTAL** and fun!

Once you've carved out half, **pull it and bullet**: extract three takeaways as bullets. Bold the first few words of each bullet as "topic titles."

Will it sometimes feel like there are more than three points to highlight? Absolutely. However, every additional bullet substantially increases the odds that people will miss one or more. When communicating, trust in the **rule of three**. As Jim Lecinski, a professor at Northwestern University's Kellogg School of Management, likes to say, "Data points don't add; they average." Including four bullets won't make your case one bit more convincing or memorable than three would—the details mush together. That's how human beings process information. Our attention is limited. The discipline of the rule of three ensures that the most compelling bits land. It's better to add a link for more information on subtopics than cram five or seven bullets into a single email.

Also, make sure to test. If your email is going to twenty or more people, take the time to run it by a handful of stakeholders for feedback. This effort pays off exponentially as the size of your intended audience grows.

The rule of three applies whether you're designing a presentation slide, creating a strategy doc, or just speaking up in a meeting. For slide decks, for example, get your points across using three slides with at least 30 percent white space on each one. You'll be shocked by how much more people retain.

Remember, if you don't distill your message, your audience may forget all of it. (To be more succinct in your verbal communication, try "delete the octopus," a tactic you can learn in six minutes at **wildcourage book.com/resources**. There, you can also find examples of how to shorten emails with the **pull it and bullet** method.)

LET THE TREE FALL

When you're overwhelmed, the conventional wisdom is to sort everything by urgency and importance, then delegate or delay smaller items. But why sort the small stuff when the big stuff is right in front of you?

Go do that thing.

Delegating takes effort. Delaying postpones the inevitable. What a waste! Deferring and delaying will never be as efficient as dropping minor tasks altogether. Be **BRUTAL** about it. You can do this safely more often than you realize.

The age-old question goes: When a tree falls in the forest and there's no one around to hear it, does it make a sound? Spoiler alert: it doesn't matter. The next time you're handed something that isn't worth *anyone's* time, **let the tree fall**. Give yourself permission to skip things that don't need doing (without telling anyone else).

For example, instead of delivering the seven action items your boss mentioned in your weekly one-on-one, pick the two or three items that really matter and obsess over them. Put all your energy into nailing them, and let the small trees quietly disappear. Don't delegate them. Don't delay them. Just *don't*.

Take minor items handed off by a client or manager, for example. Bosses often brainstorm out loud, rattling off long lists of tasks without adding that crucial preface: "One thing we *might* try is . . ." Managers often repeat their bosses' ideas without bothering to filter. Personally, when meeting with my team, I mentioned many nice-to-haves that weren't critical. I'd usually forget them by the next meeting. When I'm really jazzed about a project, many things that might boost the odds of success come to mind. Though I'd try to sort them by importance, my team understood that these ideas never share the same level of urgency. I trusted their discretion in deciding where to invest their efforts. If something really mattered, I'd follow up.

You can always put the ball back in your manager's court instead of letting the tree fall. Type everything they tell you to do, prioritize the items, and then review the list with your manager to confirm that you're on the same page. They'll likely realize a bunch of stuff can be scratched from the list. Doing this will *feel* safer, but is it really less dangerous than the **BRUTAL** approach? Isn't it just wasting more of everyone's time? Use your best judgment. There are times when asking your boss to help prioritize is perfectly fine. Just remember there are times when you can make these calls yourself and reap the benefit of doing so.

In **RECKLESS**, we will learn to calibrate risks objectively instead of emotionally. One way to do this is by comparing worst-case scenarios. For example, if your manager brings a "fallen tree" to your attention, point to the more important work you did instead: "I was just getting our Q4 sales presentation ready, which was our top priority—I'll tackle that task now." That's the worst-case scenario. And a very unlikely one. Priorities change quickly in the workplace.

What's the worst-case scenario when you constantly seek permission to prioritize? Managers hand off tasks when they're overwhelmed. If you always need hand-holding to move forward, you risk convincing them that handing off work to you is *too much work*. That conclusion leads nowhere good for your career.

NAP (not actually promotable) work, first discussed in **SELFISH**, is an excellent target for this. Tasks that aren't part of your job description and won't advance your career must be limited to 15 percent of your time at work, even if they help keep the team functioning and projects on track. Examples: taking notes in the meeting, organizing the off-site, planning the team dinner, scheduling a VP's day in your office location, leading the well-being pillar, and so on. Instead of getting it handled by a dedicated admin, organizations often subtly or unconsciously pressure female employees to tackle NAP work, but no one in the modern workplace is immune.

Review your tasks and write down everything you've been asked to do that isn't explicitly a part of your job description. Moving forward, add to that list of **NAP traps** whenever you're given a task that needs doing but *not necessarily by you*. Keep this list where you will see it when deciding priorities. If someone hands you something on that list, smile, nod, and consider letting the tree fall in *your* forest. Someone else can plant it in theirs.

Be **BRUTAL**. When the team requests NAP help, keep your hand down and sit with the discomfort until someone else volunteers. Yes, you had a blast planning last year's off-site. *Let someone else enjoy it this year.* NAP work is often necessary, fun, or beneficial to the culture, but it doesn't move the business; moving the business is what moves your career.

To be clear, letting the tree fall isn't equivalent to "quiet quitting." That's just indiscriminately leaning out of your job. Disengaging with work only leaves you more disengaged, sapping your motivation further and accelerating a downward spiral that will culminate in termination. In contrast, letting trees fall helps you devote more time and energy to the trees that have deeper roots in the business. While it may feel uncomfortable not to do Every Single Thing, you'll find that people who excel habitually say no to the small without explicitly refusing a task or wasting time arguing priorities. They just put their bandwidth into one or two essentials and *gently* evade the rest.

Here's why this works:

1. There is no end to the work that *could* be done.

2. No one will ever weigh the best use of your time as well as you can.

3. As quantity goes down, quality goes up, and people can't argue with results.

Hanging your hat on two or three significant accomplishments each quarter always beats going an inch deep on everything. Keep knocking high-value, high-visibility deliverables out of the park with **BRUTAL** efficiency, and people will get comfortable letting minor stuff slide. Eventually, they'll realize they shouldn't give you work that isn't worth your time and hand it to those who don't deliver on the big stuff as effectively. This is how you become indispensable while simultaneously avoiding overwhelm and overwork. Ironically, the people who try to do everything stay invisible—then burn out.

TRAIT TRAPS

Kind, friendly . . . and BRUTAL

Here's the obvious guardrail around being **BRUTAL**: *don't be a jerk about it!*

Serving your own needs can sometimes appear to threaten the needs of others. For example, resting for a few minutes while helping a friend move furniture might temporarily frustrate your eager-to-finish partner. They might have more endurance than you—or the bad habit of pushing themselves to exhaustion. Regardless of how they might react, *rest when you're tired*. They certainly won't be happy if you pass out because you've exceeded *your* limits, and *they don't know what it feels like to be in your body*. You've got to look out for yourself.

That said, keep your statement of needs friendly, even if the response you expect won't be. Detach with kindness and set your boundary: "Whew! That was heavy. I'm going to sit down for five minutes and rest." There's no need to be passive-aggressive: "Boy, you sure own a lot of stuff!" Just explain what you intend to do for yourself, and then do it. Even better, show some thought for them: "You must be exhausted, too. Want some of my water?" Being **BRUTAL** and kind are not mutually exclusive.

Invert your pyramid

On a flight home back to Colorado with my family, I experienced a sudden, crippling pain on my left side. Take your pick of metaphor: hot knives, sizzling electricity. Doesn't matter. It was sheer agony. We went from the airport directly to the ER, where I was diagnosed with kidney stones. *Ten* kidney stones. Ten sharpened little hate boulders. And all ten wanted *out*.

Kidney stones? Despite the intense pain, I couldn't help but giggle. How do you get kidney stones in your early forties when you eat a healthy diet and hike almost daily? Initially, I blamed my condition on the stress of trying to balance everything in my hectic life. But, as I learned, stress doesn't cause kidney stones. Dehydration does.

My doctor told me to start tracking my water intake. As it turned out, I routinely drank as little as half a liter a day—less than a fifth of the recommended amount. (Drinking more water isn't the main point here, but if you take nothing else from this book, DRINK MORE WA-TER.) As more lands on my plate, I struggle more with self-care—which is simply self-compassion in action.

Compassion is simple and obvious. "Here, friend, you look thirsty. Have a glass of water." Self-compassion is "I'm going to refill my water bottle even if it makes me a few minutes late to that Zoom call."

For me, directing compassion inward doesn't come naturally. In that, I'm not alone. Self-compassion feels abstract and, therefore, ignorable when I'm under pressure to meet hard deadlines and achieve real-world objectives. This is true even though the consequences of neglecting my needs are as concrete as *ten quarter-inch-wide jagged little chunks of minerals and salts trapped in my urinary tract.* Beyond the stones, skipping self-care measurably lowers our efficacy in other areas. We don't perform at our best when we don't get what we need. The kidney stones were just life's umpteenth reminder of that simple fact.

Maslow's pyramid-shaped hierarchy of needs places bodily requirements like food, water, and shelter at the bottom, love and belonging in the middle, and self-actualization at the top. Unfortunately, this conveys a false impression of stability. As living creatures, we aren't stable. A night of poor sleep or a missed meal can disrupt a job or relationship. A few minor issues with that bottom layer can topple the whole pyramid, especially if they coincide: inadequate sleep when you're sick, etc. To drive this point home, flip the pyramid on its head:

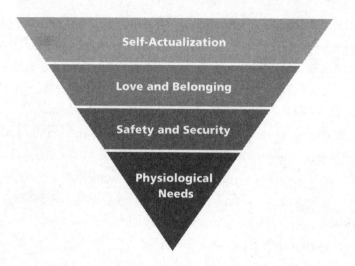

Keep this upside-down pyramid of needs in mind as you allocate your time and energy. Notice how tippy it is. Those are *needs* at the bottom, not just wants! Because of factors ranging from guilt to ambition to social pressure, your brain will tell you to ignore your needs to focus on what "matters" (as though your well-being doesn't!). If the tip of the upside-down pyramid cracks, the edifice will come down, sinking safety and security (the steady job, the mortgage on the house), love and belonging (relationships, spouse, kids), and self-actualization (the master's degree, the piano lessons). A serious medical problem is one of the many ways we're reminded of this fact, but many of us manage to remain deluded even after the fainting spell or heart attack.

For years, it's been popular for business experts to advocate for self-care. At most organizations, however, people continue to martyr themselves at the altar of work. Not only is this approach shortsighted regarding mental and physical health, it's also bad for business.

"But, Jenny, I actually have to attend all these meetings," I hear you thinking. "They're too important to miss." Is that how you add value at your company? Just by being in the room, like a mascot? At Google, I was paid for my experience and expertise. I couldn't deliver on that if I was a wreck.

On one particularly busy day, I decided to attend every meeting in its entirety, no matter how unimportant. As a result, I showed up increasingly frazzled to each one, bulldozing through agenda items without pausing long enough for a single fresh perspective. I didn't just leave my best self at home, I also impeded the efforts of my colleagues. People wanted Jenny Wood at those meetings, not that irritable grouch with a twitching eyelid.

Prioritize your basic needs: food, water, sleep, rest, exercise, and, yes, silence. If you struggle to incorporate self-care into your busiest days, add these essentials to your calendar in advance so that you can't be added to meetings during those crucial intervals. If necessary, set alarms to remind yourself when it's time to take care of yourself, whether drinking a glass of water or walking around the block and getting some fresh air. Make self-care as automatic as possible because, like me, you might not remember to take care of yourself when the pressure's on.

―――――――――

Less is more. **BRUTAL** frees up time, energy, and mental bandwidth. What do we do with those reserves once we free them? Take big leaps. It's time to get **RECKLESS**.

BRUTAL:
Draw lines and stick to them

- **Permission granted.** Escape the trap of *performative* work by focusing on *rewardative* work that moves the ball forward. If an investment of time isn't paying off, leave at intermission.

- **Don't cry over spilled email.** Instead of chasing the mirage of an empty inbox, filter what doesn't matter, focus on email during specific blocks of time each day, and check your feelings before hastily responding to important emails.

- **Let the tree fall.** Skip unimportant tasks quietly. If they're actually necessary, they'll come around again, and you'll have been busy doing unambiguously important work in the meantime.

- **Kind, friendly . . . and BRUTAL.** Don't be a jerk when setting boundaries. Just set them and move on. You can be unapologetic about your needs while also being thoughtful. Clear *is* kind.

- **Invert your pyramid.** Prioritize your basic needs, like food, water, and rest, because they're the foundation of everything goal-related.

8

RECKLESS

Err on the side of action

> **Reckless**
>
> **(adj.):** marked by lack of proper caution.
>
> **Reckless redefined:** The courage to take calculated risks.

After Titi Akinsanmi, a Google employee, used Own Your Career advice to land a coveted role, she sent me unsolicited positive feedback about the program. The program had helped get her promoted, and it made my day. Because I was in a hurry, I pasted her two-sentence note verbatim into the subject line of an email and forwarded it to the handful of people working on OYC with me at the time. It wouldn't have made much sense to anyone else: just Akinsanmi's name followed by a few casual words of praise. Nothing in the body of the email. This was OK in the context of our little team. My colleagues would recognize this as a forwarded testimonial. You probably use a shorthand when texting friends, family, and close colleagues.

After clicking send on the email, I returned to what I'd been working on for another few seconds before my intuition pinged me. Going back to my Gmail tab, I realized, to my horror, that I'd sent this cryptic email to the entire OYC mailing list: at the time, over twenty-seven thousand Google employees, including more than a few in the C-suite.

"No, no, no," I muttered to myself, moving the pointer to click unsend just as the window to do so expired.

"To err is human," the English writer Alexander Pope wrote. "To forgive divine." I wonder whether Pope would categorize *self*-forgiveness as equally transcendent. Being **RECKLESS** is about getting comfortable making all the low-risk, high-reward moves that drive progress in work and life. It's an absolutely essential **Trait** because second-guessing every potential action saps momentum—scrutinize everything you might out of misguided perfectionism, and you'll never take enough swings at bat to score a run. In my case, the move was forwarding a testimonial to boost morale. In yours, it might be reaching out to a former colleague to catch up over coffee, sending a cold pitch to a potential client, or throwing an idea out in a large meeting. In all these cases, the most challenging part isn't facing the consequences of failure, which are rarely life and death. It's the harsh way we treat ourselves in those rare but inevitable moments when things do go awry.

Staring at my screen helplessly, arms tingling, face flushed, stomach in turmoil, I said some things to myself I would never utter to another human being. Not only had I annoyed tens of thousands of people with an unwanted email, but I'd also sent them something baffling. My slapdash, cryptic message represented the opposite of the sleek, buttoned-up OYC brand we'd all worked hard to build.

If Warren Buffett said it takes twenty years to build a reputation and five minutes to destroy one, I'd beat the record tenfold. You only get thirty seconds to unsend a Gmail message.

We take risks every minute of every day. Even an email represents a roll of the dice. You can't pursue what you want effectively if you hesitate and deliberate before every potential hazard. Rethinking every move to avoid failure at any cost guarantees that whatever you're chasing will be long gone by the time you get there.

To thrive, have the wild courage to be a little **RECKLESS**. Personal and professional growth demands the ability to weigh risks objectively, take risks regularly, and tolerate all the inevitable failures stoically.

Yes, safeguards matter. I check my "To:" lines more carefully now. But you must accustom yourself to failure and the process of *recovery* from failure. The fall *and* the bounce. Proving to yourself that you can recover from occasional scrapes is the only way you'll move fast enough to get where you're going in this lifetime.

"Everyone makes mistakes," I told myself as my heart rate slowed. "It's fine." After repeating this a few times as a kind of mantra, and after the wind that had been knocked out of me returned, I began to believe myself . . . a little bit.

IN DEFENSE OF HEALTHY RECKLESSNESS

If you're on the fence, do it. If you don't act on passion and excitement immediately, they fade. If you do, they can give you the strength and focus to compensate for insufficient forethought. Anyway, most forethought is fear-thought: rather than planning out a strategy, you're just weighing worst-case scenarios against each other with no thought to their relative likelihood.

Don't let yourself become trapped pondering the options to death. There are too many possible paths in this big, crazy world. Given the option between endless deliberation and imperfect preparation, err on the side of action. Perfection is impossible.

I call this bias toward action being **RECKLESS**. If the word feels a little dangerous, that's good. It should. It's a powerful, life-changing tool to apply judiciously, not carelessly. We don't just take risks. We weigh them based on the available data and make an informed call within a reasonable timeframe.

Research shows that you regret a negative outcome more when caused by a lack of action. In other words, you regret the moves you *don't* make more than the negative consequences of the ones you do. Failure is always possible, but it *feels* worse when it happens because you were sitting on your thumbs.

There were several points during my career when I could have done a year or two working on an international project abroad. I regret not seizing one of those opportunities—it would have been an amazing life experience for my family and me. However, most of the failures we regret aren't so momentous. Like wishing you'd clarified what a manager meant when they said something vague or used a tone of voice you couldn't interpret . . . and let it eat away at you for an entire weekend. These little failures to act add up.

We fail to be sufficiently **RECKLESS** when we overestimate the risk of failure and the significance of the consequences. To the fragile ego, any failure is unacceptable. This unwillingness to take smart risks limits our growth. Successful people fail far *more* than most people do. If you want what they have, don't ignore the discography to focus on the hit albums. The road to every significant achievement is absolutely littered with missteps.

To double your success, quadruple your failure rate.

Stop waiting for the sound of the ball hitting the catcher's mitt to decide whether you *should* have taken the swing. More swings mean more strikes *and* more hits. Meanwhile, swinging regularly improves your intuition about when to swing. When it comes to people, opportunities, and ideas, well-honed intuition beats any amount of deliberation. Scrutinize the fine print on a mortgage with due diligence, but when it comes to life's big decisions, like marrying that special someone, taking a big job in a new country, or starting your first business, trust your gut to lead you. No list of pros and cons will get you closer to the truth without incorporating a degree of intuition.

Accepting or even leaning into the possibility of failure is scary, especially for those of us who excelled in school and fought like mad to turn every A-minus into an A. Bestselling author and veteran blogger Seth Godin brings a **RECKLESS** mindset to his writing: "Half of my blog posts are below average, I get that, but I don't know which half." Instead of fruitlessly pursuing some idea of perfection, Godin continues to write and publish. Having done so steadily for decades, he has developed a vast body of work whose lower half easily beats the upper half of many other business thinkers.

Half of everything you did this week was below your average, too. That's just math. If you wrote a hundred emails, fifty were worse than your average. Fifty below-average emails!

This isn't chilling but freeing! Half of what you do is below your bar on any given day, no matter how high you raise the bar. You're not perfect. You never will be. You can't be ten out of ten on everything, nor does it make sense to optimize for perfection. If I worry endlessly about whether this paragraph of the book will be flawless, I'll never finish writing it and start the next one. Allowing some of my work to land in the "meh" category helps me work faster and more fearlessly. That means I can do more, improving more quickly while creating more opportunities for lightning to strike. Pretty good work is great if it's *consistent*.

The amount of rejection, disappointment, frustration, delay, and, yes, failure that a highly successful person must learn to face is staggering. Failure and loss are inextricable from getting what you want. If you can't counteract *impact bias*, the cognitive tendency to overestimate how unpleasant a future failure will feel and how long it will last, you'll never fail enough to succeed at the highest level. You'll never be properly **RECKLESS**. A mentor of mine, tech VP Rob McClung, shared something his father, Jim, told him: "If you don't have a few fouls, you're not really in the game."

No one is born with a **RECKLESS** mindset. It's a choice. Embarrassment and humiliation affected me *deeply* as a kid. Eventually, I recognized that being thin-skinned was an obstacle. How would I chase my dreams from a position of permanent cringe? I started challenging myself, doing harmless but scary things to build my tolerance.

When Stef, my best friend in high school, dared me to stand on a table at the frozen yogurt place and sing "My Country, 'Tis of Thee," I got up there and belted out all four stanzas.

"You're such a nut, Jenny!" another friend, Vic, said after I warbled the final "to thee I siiiiiiiing."

Why'd I do it? To show myself that I wouldn't die. It was practice.

You get fewer double-dog dares as you exit adolescence, but practice opportunities are everywhere. I've been responsible for some cringeworthy humdingers during my adult life. By framing them as opportunities for spine straightening and skin toughening, I've pushed through them successfully and developed a knack for bouncing back.

Do I welcome embarrassment? No! But I've made peace with the possibility. In the body and brain, excitement and fear can feel the same. Cortisol and adrenaline get released. Breathing and heart rate accelerate. We *interpret* these sensations based on our mindset. My heart thumping in my ribs before a **RECKLESS** move tells me *I care about the results*. That's the mindset I *choose*. The swing mattered, regardless of whether I missed.

Isn't that the point of life, to work on what matters, win or lose?

We don't weigh our early life decisions properly. When we're young, we don't yet realize that it can take a few false starts to land on the ideal career or perfect partner. As a result, we play it far too safe while navigating work and relationships. Youth is all about taking big swings. You learn much faster that way, and the risks are smaller than you think. Loosen up! Nothing is fixed in stone. Keep moving. Better to try, fail, and try something else than default to the safest possible bet.

Age doesn't help, either. Later in life, we look back at our younger selves and decide we should have leaped instead of looked. Meanwhile, we doubt our ability to switch careers or try new ventures. "I had plenty of time to start a business back then," the forty-year-old thinks. "Too bad I *really* don't have the option now." Just wait until you're sixty looking back at forty.

We're always ready to take risks in hindsight, never realizing that today will be yesterday when tomorrow comes. Start *now*. As the saying goes, the best time to plant a tree is thirty years ago. The second best time is today.

We must recalibrate our risk radar to get **RECKLESS**. As the great choreographer George Balanchine always told his dancers: "What are you saving it for? You might be dead tomorrow!"

USE THE DIFFICULTY

Cleanup on aisle three! Pretending I hadn't sent a random email to a good chunk of Google wouldn't solve anything. Once I'd calmed down, I sent a short follow-up email apologizing to the mailing list. You can't move on from a mess without acknowledging your part. Second, I reached out to Akinsanmi, whose testimonial had "gone viral." Titi didn't deserve to have her name attached to my mistake.

"Actually," she wrote back, "I've received several emails congratulating me on the promotion." My blunder had been a *good* thing, she assured me. In the hours that followed, I received over fifty reassuring replies from colleagues:

> I know this must be incredibly stressful for you, but I promise, no one cares or is paying attention. People will delete it and move on. This is only stressful for you, no one else.

Success at *anything* requires doing a lot of *something*: pitching, submitting, speaking, writing, etc. Mistakes are inevitable when you do something a lot, no matter how many precautions you take. Perfection isn't an option; it's a direction, not a destination. All you can do is minimize mistakes, get comfortable with the idea of making mistakes, and, in some cases, *use* your mistakes once you've made them. All you can do is get **RECKLESS**.

Forwarding a positive testimonial is a good action. I screwed it up, but that doesn't mean the decision to forward was flawed. Nor did my mistake mean I needed to scrutinize every future email under a microscope. If I did that, I wouldn't have been able to function. As a Google leader, I sent several hundred emails a week. No time for microscopes.

You can seek perfection or progress. Not both. And, unlike perfection, progress is possible.

Sir Michael Caine learned to leverage mistakes as a young theater actor in England. The company was rehearsing a scene. At the end of an improvisation between two of his fellow actors, Sir Michael was to enter the scene through a door. Unfortunately, one of the actors threw a chair during the improvisation, which lodged in the door, preventing Sir Michael's entrance.

Poking his head through the gap, Sir Michael called out to the director: "I'm sorry, sir, I can't get in."

"Use the difficulty!" the director said.

"What do you mean?" the young actor replied, still struggling to free the door from the chair.

"If it's a comedy, *fall* over it. If it's a drama, pick it up and *smash* it."

Live theater, folks. As in work and life, things will go wrong no matter how much you practice and prepare. The show must go on, so figure out how to leverage what the problem gives you. *Using* the difficulty instead of complaining about it or pretending it isn't there some-times leads to exciting and creative choices that surpass your original aim.

In the next Own Your Career newsletter I wrote, I used my diffi-culty, explaining the five-step process I'd followed to REACT to my mistake and overcome it.

1. **Recognize** that not everything you do will be perfect.

2. **Empower** yourself to own it quickly and clean it up. Then take a deep breath. It happens to everyone.

3. **Apologize** directly to those involved.

4. **Celebrate** the unexpected goodness that comes out of a mistake.

5. **Trust** that your fellow employees will have your back.

To my surprise, this became my all-time most popular newsletter. People could relate! The advice helped other people cope with failure productively. Somehow, my most embarrassing day at Google delivered one of my biggest career wins.

Instead of dwelling on how bad failure will feel, ask yourself how you will *use the difficulty* if you do fail, engaging the planning part of the brain instead. It's a small but powerful shift to a more **RECKLESS** mindset. (I've included a simple but powerful exercise to turn failures and mis-takes into wins—or at least lessons—at **wildcouragebook.com/resources**. You can use it to reframe future decisions and risks, too.)

MOVE, THEN MAP

You'll never feel ready, and that's a good thing. If you feel 100 percent prepared for the task ahead, you're headed down the path of boredom no matter where it leads. You might reach your goal, but it will be too easy to feel like a genuine victory. More likely, you'll lose interest long before you get there.

When you're **RECKLESS**, every task should challenge you to some extent. That's how you keep growing. We experience depression and even burnout in the pursuit of too-easy objectives. Stop swimming laps in the kiddie pool and seek out the deep end to discover your motivation and purpose. That little shiver of fear before you dive in is a sign you're in the right spot.

Planning and preparation matter, but don't use them to postpone uncertainty and fear. You don't have to be the world's expert to *start*. (How did the expert earn their expertise besides doing the thing first— and badly?) You don't need a ten-year plan complete with charts, graphs, and milestones to stick a toe in the water. That's just one more way we defer the discomfort of getting started. I ran a LinkedIn poll that confirmed my suspicions: 81 percent of 2,500 respondents didn't have a ten-year plan, and 67 percent didn't even have a five-year plan. It's something people talk about but rarely do.

Want to publish a novel? Before buying ten books on writing or quitting your job and joining an MFA program, sit down for ten minutes of writing *right now*. How does it feel? Uncomfortable, right? Good. Do it for ten minutes every day this week. It may not sound like it, but this is as **RECKLESS** as it gets. You're erring on the side of action, taking calculated risks in pursuit of your goal.

Want to start a solo consultancy? Instead of building a website, researching pricing, and studying negotiation, seek one freelance consulting gig by contacting former colleagues. Use one of countless consulting agreement templates available online. Get out there and try it instead of burrowing down the rabbit hole. Make some mistakes and learn from them.

Move, *then* map. That magical feeling of knowing you're ready will never come if you wait for it. Movement *makes* the magic. Action, not thinking, provides clarity.

Yes, I struggle with this. My friend Taylor and I went for a hike on a trip to Montana. Because I wasn't familiar with the area, I felt anxious to complete the "perfect" hike. I wanted to pick the *best* path, so when we passed a park ranger, I bombarded her with questions: "How far is the lake? What's the incline? Is one trail muddier than the other? Which view is nicer at the end? Are they doing active forest work on this trail? Do you recommend the out-and-back or the loop?" Looking up, I saw that Taylor was already well ahead of me.

"Jenny, it's *all* gorgeous," she shouted without pausing. "Let's go!"

Remember, default to action.

What is the smallest step forward that you could take right now? What would feel scary today but fill you with pride tomorrow? That's the **RECKLESS** move.

When we're insecure and uncertain, we consistently get the balance between preparation and action wrong. Worse, we tell ourselves that we're being careful or even strategic when we're being cowardly. This isn't about betting everything you own on red. It's about moving and mapping in tandem. Taking one small, smart risk after another. Coping with occasional failures. Making gradual but steady improvement.

Business development expert Terry Rice said, "Time kills deals." Rice was referring to business deals with others. In that sense, he's absolutely right. Write back same day when locking in a partnership, sale, or deal. People respond to speed. To close the deal, act fast, even if you haven't vetted your email with five specialists.

However, time kills *all* deals, even the deals we make with ourselves. Our resolutions: "I'm going to get to the gym every day before work," or "I'm going to make the C-suite by forty," or "I'm going to find a good therapist and get to work on these issues." When we resolve to take action toward an objective, we do so because we're experiencing a surge of motivation. Maybe we huffed a little too much after climbing a flight of stairs. Maybe we realized we've been coasting in our career. Maybe we blew up at our partner for reasons we still can't articulate. Whatever the source of motivation, use it. Motivation fades in a day or two. The only way to lock in that momentum is action. Today. Go.

TRAIT TRAPS

Take a dance break

The difference was palpable when "Steve" took over a senior leadership role connected to mine by a dotted line. Steve's predecessor had been an active and engaged leader who checked in with us regularly, offering a friendly ear and, when requested, guidance and support. Steve, in contrast, stayed in his office, door closed. At first, I assumed he was busy getting oriented, but a few weeks later, it became clear this was Steve's normal approach.

Because I was junior to Steve, my stomach didn't like the idea of a confrontation, but my head told me to take the risk. Steve's success as a leader mattered to the organization's success, which mattered to my success. It was time to be a little **RECKLESS**.

However, before I had given it any real thought, I found myself in the work kitchen with Steve himself—and no bystanders. *Perfect.* I couldn't resist the temptation of checking one unpleasant task off my list. Cornering Steve as he poured himself a bowl of cereal and without any forethought on how to phrase my feedback, I suggested he walk the floor more often to connect with the team as his predecessor had done. Nodding curtly, Steve retreated to his office, closing the door behind him with an audible thunk.

Oof. I immediately spotted three ways I'd mishandled that action in my haste.

First, wrong time and place. Serious feedback should be delivered in a scheduled one-on-one, not sprung on someone pouring cereal in the kitchen. Second, I hadn't read the room first to see whether Steve was open to feedback. Third, I'd compared him unfavorably to his predecessor. No wonder he left in such a hurry!

Don't confuse speed and sloppiness. **RECKLESS** is about deciding and moving swiftly; it's *not* a license to rush important tasks when you've got a full plate. Broaching the subject was a valid choice, but acting without preparation was not. Five minutes of forethought would have transformed my results.

Sometimes, it feels as if we're on someone else's timeline. Being **RECKLESS** is about pushing through your natural resistance to healthy risks, not rushing into a commitment to please others. For example, when a hiring manager makes a job offer, we feel as though we must respond immediately. Yes, trust your instincts on big decisions, but you can nearly always make time to think things through. Ideally, sleep on any significant decision where you feel external pressure to comply. If an idea feels right late at night *and* early the following day, it's probably sound. And, if sleep isn't an option, insist on a short period of reflection, even if it feels absolutely impossible.

While working at Harvard Business School, I helped with a research project under negotiations expert Michael Wheeler. We found that simply taking a few minutes alone before a crucial decision improved outcomes. Call it a *dance break*. Every negotiation is a dance; sometimes, you must step away from the dance floor, take a breath, and get some perspective. Letting the other side pressure you to move forward leads to poor results.

I've been in plenty of situations where I felt as if I *had* to respond that instant. That's not being **RECKLESS**. That's fight-or-flight mode. That sense of urgency is a signal to buy yourself a little time. Tell someone there's an important call on the other line and that you'll call them back. Be **BRUTAL** with this. Schedule a follow-up meeting. Step out of the room for a few minutes because your "kid" called. Take a dance break.

Pride lies

Fear adds friction, slowing our progress without actually helping us minimize risk. **RECKLESS** means getting comfortable with a certain proportion of low-stakes failure in pursuit of growth, orienting yourself toward the high-discomfort but low-*actual*-risk actions that propel you toward your goals.

However, pride can also make it difficult to judge risk and reward. When our ego is on the line, we will do genuinely reckless things without a glance at the precipice beneath. Fear pushes us to play things too safe. Pride pushes us to risk our necks for nothing. Occasionally, my pride tries to kill me. I'll give you two examples, although I could probably give two hundred.

After months of gradually increasing my weekly running mileage before a marathon, I was told to run a max of only twenty miles as my longest training run the final two weeks and taper down from that. This gives your body time to rest and recover before the big race. After scoring a coveted lottery spot in the New York City Marathon, I decided to do the Denver half-marathon two weeks prior as my final, twenty-mile training run: two miles to the starting line, thirteen miles in the race, and five more alone when I'd finished.

Once the race started, I matched pace with a lovely older gentleman who planned to run the full marathon that day. The guy had three decades and about fifty marathons on me. Watching him breeze along mile after mile, my pride started talking to me. The idea of peeling off from the race halfway through suddenly lost its appeal.

"Boy," I thought to myself. "This guy is a great running buddy." A mile later: "I'm having fun—this race is going by so quickly." Another two miles: "Heck, what would happen if I ran the whole thing?" Pride worked double time to frame this idiotic notion as a good idea. The rationalizations poured forth: What if my flight got canceled and I missed the NYC marathon? What if bad weather meant I couldn't finish? By completing Denver, I could check a marathon off my bucket list *no matter what.*

So I kept running despite everything I'd learned about marathon training. My pride told me I could do it all.

Later that day, as they draped the finisher's medal around my neck,

I noticed a slight twinge in my left foot. Limping back to the car, I realized I might have made a mistake. By mile two of the New York City Marathon, I knew I had. My foot was screaming in pain, but that was OK because it was numb by then at the end of the Verrazzano Bridge. While I completed the race, it took *a year and a half* to recover from that *completely avoidable* injury.

But that's just a chronic, painful injury. Pride can do worse. For example, I went out for a flight shortly after getting my pilot's license for visual flight rules. A VFR license means you aren't qualified to fly on instruments alone. Taxiing my favorite Cessna 152 to the runway under an ominous sky, I called my flight instructor. Was it too cloudy this morning?

"Seems risky," she said, "but it's your call."

That's right, pride said. It's *my* call, and *I'm a pilot now*. Rationalizations: I'd already paid for the aircraft. I'd woken up at the crack of dawn. I'd spent forty minutes of meticulous prep before lugging *an entire plane* out of the hangar by myself—a bear of a job, even with a tow bar.

Pride blinding me to the risk, I called the tower for takeoff clearance. The air traffic controller gave it to me but mentioned the low cloud ceiling and visibility as a not-so-subtle cue to reconsider. I did not. Legally, I could fly—barely. Besides, playing it safe is for amateurs. I was a licensed pilot!

Within a minute of takeoff, I was enshrouded by clouds. As a VFR pilot, I'd been trained to fly using the ground to orient myself, and now I couldn't see it. I'd never flown with a canvas of white covering every window. In over my head and terrified, I discovered that heart-pounding anxiety made it hard to think clearly. As my breathing intensified, I realized I couldn't make sense of the heading, altitude, and airspeed readings on the flight controls. I thought of my fiancé, Jon, and my parents. I was going to die.

Thankfully, I didn't let pride prevent me from asking for help. The air traffic controller talked me through the landing step-by-step, and thanks to his professionalism, I was safe on the ground before I knew it.

For the rest of the morning, adrenaline and cortisol coursed through my system. In the office that day, I kept flashing back to that sudden canvas of white, the utter confusion and helplessness I'd felt. This embarrassing and scary episode continues to shape how I handle risk in my decision-making.

Many times in life, the bold, scary move is the right one. Yes, take that opportunity to study or work abroad even though you don't know the language (yet). Yes, take that unexpected operations role to diversify your résumé from accounting. Yes, go on a third date even when the second wasn't "perfect." However, always listen to your gut. Learn from each risk. Seek that line between minor fears you should ignore and major ones you should absolutely heed. Remember the difference between not acting out of fear and acting out of pride.

While rising to leadership requires a tolerance for risk, winning a coveted position can make us intensely risk averse. Putting everything on the line is easier when you don't have much to lose. Once you've achieved a long-sought goal, the challenge is to stay **RECKLESS** enough to keep pushing and growing.

In the next chapter, we will explore the trait that, in many ways, calls on every other: **Bossiness**. It's time to inspire wild courage in others.

RECKLESS
Err on the side of action

- **Use the difficulty.** Instead of pretending you didn't make a mistake, own it, apologize, and then leverage a silver lining.

- **Move, then map.** Don't use planning and research to postpone action and learning. Experiments provide data, and data informs decisions. This ensures you're never far off course. Put ten minutes a day toward concrete action when starting something new.

- **Take a dance break.** Don't confuse speed with sloppiness—always take a quiet moment before important decisions. The more someone pressures you to decide, the more important you take the time to think it over.

- **Pride lies.** Aim for smart, calculated risks—don't let your ego get you in hot water. If that inner voice says, "It'll be fine," get a second opinion.

9

BOSSY
Steer others to success

> **Bossy**
>
> **(adj.):** inclined to domineer; dictatorial.
>
> **Bossy redefined:** The courage to listen and lead.

After a decade of climbing the ranks at Google, I reached the point of managing other managers. Despite the company's apparent confidence in me, I struggled with performance anxiety. A decade in the trenches didn't guarantee my potential for upper management. Could I deliver at the same level with significantly more people in my org?

A flight back to Boulder early in my tenure as a senior leader left me with a few hours of peace before leading an off-site the next day with a number of the managers who reported to me. We would spend a day planning a high-stakes transition, shutting down a major business unit in one part of the country and building it back up in another. With my impostor syndrome flaring, I used every trick in the book—this book—to wrangle my uncomfortable emotions and face the blank page I'd just opened with a clear head. **WEIRD:** Bring my authentic inner leader to the table. **SHAMELESS:** Own my new role. **SELFISH:** Prove my ability to the company to continue my upward climb. **OBSESSED**: Put in the prep work. Et cetera.

For the duration of the flight, I worked on the strategy we were supposed to develop the next day: our North Star mission statement, the three pillars of the transition, a leader for each one, and so on. As I resolved each area of uncertainty, my anxiety subsided, and my confidence grew. *Yes.* This *is what the team needs.* This *is how I will prove my value to the organization.* This *is Jenny Wood as boss.*

I didn't get much sleep that night, as there was still too much prep to complete. However, by the following morning, I'd completed an elaborate, thirty-slide deck outlining how the transition would work. Once I finished, I wondered whether we still needed the full day. I'd resolved every open question.

You can thank me later, folks.

When we assembled in the conference room, I plugged my laptop in and opened the first slide, crammed with answers to the problems we were supposed to solve that day. Ta-da! To my surprise, the energy in the room immediately changed. It got so quiet you could hear an erasable marker drop. However, I assumed they were busy absorbing the extraordinary quantity of leadership I'd stuffed into a single slide, so I started presenting. Once I finished blowing their minds, I smiled triumphantly and opened it up for questions.

They raked me over the coals.

I quickly learned that the whole presentation had been an insulting affront to the team.

The comments went something like this: "Why would you come here thinking you have all the answers?" one manager essentially asked me. "We were coming together as a team to tackle this problem. We bring a combined thirty-five years of experience on this team. How long have you been in this role, three *months*? Who are you to say that one of us should lead the people pillar and another should lead operations? Do you even know our strengths yet?" It sounds harsh, but that was the gist.

Another manager was more circumspect: "We appreciate your effort. However, we know this business much better than you. Why wouldn't you call on our expertise before deciding on the strategy?"

On it went. By the time everyone had said their piece, my heart was in my stomach, and my stomach was on the floor. I was mortified. That said, I knew what I had to do next.

"OK, team," I said. "My apologies. Let's scrap this plan and start over."

This was the beginning of the most difficult transition of my career. My approach at that meeting encapsulates the dark side of bossiness: insecurities run rampant. All I'd needed to do was toss a bunch of Sharpies on the table, ask a bunch of **NOSY** open-ended questions, and encourage people to contribute. Creating a safe space for ideation would have made it easier for them to bring their valuable experience, expertise, and talent to solving the problem. The whole point of a manager or leader is to bring out the best in the team. To make their jobs easier. It can feel uncomfortable for new leaders, but getting others to do the work makes you look much more effective than struggling to do everything yourself.

As an executive at Google, I learned to leverage my team's knowledge and abilities, delegate to them wherever possible, and attempt to spend more of my time listening. My leadership experience couldn't have been more different from my work as an individual contributor. That's because, unlike individual contributors, leaders aren't expected to bring answers. They're supposed to ask questions instead:

- What does the company's vision mean for our team?

- How will we execute against our mission?

- What are the key metrics to watch?

- What strengths do we bring to the table?

- What will make this meeting successful?

Your questions may differ, but the approach is universal. Leaders help *others* succeed. When I say get **BOSSY**, I mean be a genuine boss: an empathic, supportive, yet decisive leader who knows when to speak up and when to listen, when to let the team figure a problem out themselves, and when to step in with help and a fresh perspective.

As a leader, are you ready to stop inflating your ego and start lifting others instead?

IN DEFENSE OF BOSSINESS

Something happens when you keep successfully getting what you go after. People look to you for guidance. They set their bar by yours. Yes, *you*, that **WEIRD, SELFISH, SHAMELESS, OBSESSED, NOSY, MANIPULATIVE, BRUTAL**, and **RECKLESS** person who once assumed they'd be none of those things. All the **Traits** that looked so scary and negative in this book's table of contents come together to create something unique. Through a strange alchemy, they create a "natural" leader.

All the **Traits** are leadership traits, and yet all are discouraged when we're young or seen as lower in status. What's worse than being "bossy" on the playground? When embracing them pays off, however, these behaviors are regarded differently. Shamelessness transmutes into confidence. Nosiness to curiosity. Recklessness to courage.

Research shows that violating social norms signals leadership. Remember the "red sneaker effect"? Being **WEIRD**—and getting away with it—"implies that one has the power to act according to one's own volition despite situational constraints, which fuels perceptions of power." The more you put the **Traits** into practice, the higher your stock will rise.

Unfortunately, some people use the power they gain for personal ends. The shift toward self-interest spells an early end to their reign. On the other hand, leaders with longevity *double down* on the generosity that got them where they are: "How can I support you this week?" caps every weekly one-on-one meeting with a direct report. They set up office hours for employees to share ideas and ask questions. They delegate everything they can, refusing the temptation to make themselves indispensable. They praise publicly and admonish in private. Ultimately, leaders like these serve others even more than they did on their way up the ladder. As CEO, the *most* effective use of your time and energy is helping everyone else do *their* job.

Being a leader does *not* mean knowing everything or being able to do everything. When I first rose to a leadership position, I experienced impostor syndrome, exacerbated by my mistaken belief that I needed to know, see, and do all. Then I learned I was there to help my team solve problems instead of solving problems for them. A leader's most powerful tools are the Humble Two: "I don't know" and "I was wrong."

HANDS OFF THE WHEEL

You lead by helping others do their jobs more effectively instead of doing the job yourself, but it's hard to relinquish control. I became a leader at Google because of my fancy driving. Now I was supposed to let others take the wheel? Not so easy for me. I fought the idea stubbornly until a boss defused my resistance: "You get full credit for everything your team does."

Wow.

Since my promotion, I'd struggled to reconcile the desire to be seen as successful with the responsibility to help others shine. Though I understood leadership intellectually, part of me had held back, reserving the right to dive in and fix things when my team did anything differently than I would. In short, I had the whole thing backward. It wasn't either-or. It was *both*.

This meant letting go of the wheel. *Doing* the day-to-day work deserved only half my attention. The other half? *Communicating* up, down, and across. Up: sharing our accomplishments with leadership. Down: helping my team understand the larger vision driving our specific goals. Across: emailing stakeholders and peers across the organization, ensuring seamless integration of left and right hands.

If I coach my team to success, *I'm the coach of a winning team.* That's a good thing. Watch any football game, and you'll see that those potbellied old coots on the sidelines are as excited as the players after a victory. They get paid for winning seasons, not scoring touchdowns. Now that I was a sideline geezer, it was time to put down the ball and pick up the whistle.

As a leader, you're seen as a winner if you lead a team of winners. So forget about taking credit. Delegate. Bestow credit wherever it belongs. Celebrate your team's successes with the rest of the organization. Advocate for them. Name names. Turn your direct reports into heroes. The credit goes to you, too.

In your first management role, suddenly making yourself dispensable in this way feels terrifying. Until you lead a team, you succeed by convincing everyone that you are essential to getting results, as we've seen throughout the book. The organization *needs* you to do X, Y, or Z. Your ability to deliver persuaded them to put you in charge of a team. Now the game changes, however. Leaders are judged by a different metric: the ability to generate seven times as much X, Y, and Z *from others.*

No one expects a tennis pro to clean the court or fetch balls. She's there to swing a racket, not a broom. Likewise, no one expects the CEO of a Fortune 500 organization to enter Q4 data into a P&L sheet before making his decision about a make-or-break merger. For the CEO, the swing is the decision.

Being an effective leader requires serious manipulation. If you're uncomfortable building relationships and influencing others, forget about moving up. Stick to being an individual contributor. If you enjoy doing the work, you won't be satisfied helping others do the work better. You'll be in meetings or on calls. If connecting with others isn't your happy place, find ways to gain seniority and more pay without entering management. Because leaders lead. They set objectives, rally the troops, and ensure steady progress toward the goal.

Perhaps you've heard the saying that A players hire A players and B players hire C players. Don't let that bit about A players activate your impostor syndrome. If you value your job, hire, retain, and promote people who are wildly better at doing the work than you ever were. They're not competition, they're *ammunition*. Hiring people who *don't* threaten your ego (to help you achieve your objectives) is like bringing a knife to a gunfight. Don't you want to win? Your direct reports should leave you feeling outclassed—mine sure did.

BE A SET RAT

I failed at my first big team off-site largely because I hadn't spent enough time shadowing the people in my new group. Instead of talking, I should have listened. I never would have presumed to know better than my team if I had.

In Hollywood, many get their start in the movie industry not via film school but by spending time on movie sets. These "set rats" immerse themselves in filmmaking through observation and osmosis. Don't presume to sit in the director's chair until you've listened to everyone, from the gaffer to the cinematographer. As the director, you should understand their basic needs and pain points, because one of your jobs is to make theirs easier.

If you work in an office, keep your door open and spend most of your time on the other side of it. If your work is remote, use chat, video, and other online tools to keep the virtual doors open, not just between you and your team but between team members. Invest time in learning what each person does and how they prefer doing it.

As a leader, you can ask to shadow *anyone* on the org chart, whether higher or lower than you. If possible, aim for an hour of shadowing each week—an hour of being a set rat. This can involve physically sitting with an employee at their desk, sharing their screen, or listening to customer phone calls.

Your goal is *not* to critique their work but to empathize with their unique challenges and needs and figure out ways to make things work better for them. Make sure they understand that. Shadowing, you might discover your direct report uses nine different, incompatible tools to complete their weekly data analysis. Your job as a leader is to figure out how that job can be done with one. Likewise, you might learn that customers are confused by the different product offerings.

Great leaders remove friction across the team, address pain points, break ties, and help people communicate and coordinate in different parts of the business. As efficiency and serendipity improve, so do results. Obviously, the people who do the work are the experts on doing that work, so don't presume to help them do it until you understand it.

At first, I dreaded the idea of being a set rat. I didn't want to reveal my ignorance to my direct reports. However, I was forced to accept that my ignorance and efforts to hide it would be obvious. So I stopped trying and soon discovered how much value I could offer using my outsider's perspective.

Leading isn't being the expert on everything. Leading is *listening*. When we listen with empathy, we connect with people, help them with today's problems, and learn what we need to anticipate tomorrow's problems. For example, a few hours in the trenches might reveal that the workday is more grueling than you had estimated. Those sales quotas or software delivery milestones might need recalibration. Often, productivity increases when we *decrease* targets. Unrealistic expectations create chaos and drain morale. Adjust expectations, and people stop wasting time and energy gaming the metrics. Move the goalposts within reach, and results improve.

Being a set rat isn't easy. This is not just because you must swallow your pride and put yourself in a vulnerable place. Because shadowing others is never urgent, it takes willpower to schedule it and follow through. However, the results are more than worthwhile.

PATTERNS, NOT PROBLEMS

People focus on problems, and managers are no exception. Unfortunately, putting out fires all the time leaves no bandwidth to notice, let alone address, that the building itself is a tinderbox. Rather than get to the root of things, managers scurry from one mess to the next, cleaning things up, cursing their bad luck, and wondering why their leadership isn't more effective.

"I solve for patterns, not problems," my colleague Jen McGann once told me. This is what great leaders like Jen do. While the team solves individual problems, they step back from the trees and observe the forest.

I'm sure you're nodding along. Pattern seeking makes sense in theory, and nearly any leader will claim they prefer that approach. However, the practice of actually seeking patterns remains murky. Problems feel so urgent. They demand a response, even if that response amounts to running back and forth, waving your arms in the air, and going, "Aahhhhhh!" (If you've worked at the average company, you've observed managers doing what amounts to this.) As leaders, we like sober judgment and deliberate strategy as concepts but often struggle to make the leap from problem solver to pattern spotter.

Sticking to a step-by-step process will help turn an abstract notion into a daily habit. Consider the following example: At the quarterly roundtable with the VP and some individual contributors, a sales rep announces that customers are complaining about the new red widgets. Apparently, some find them much harder to install than the old green ones.

"We don't want unhappy customers," the VP knee-jerks. "Stop selling the red widgets. Let's put all our energy into selling the green widgets instead. Those have been around much longer, and no one ever complains about the installation process." Problem solved.

Or is it?

———

Next time you're tempted by the relief offered by a quick and easy fix to a pressing problem, QUASH it.

Quantify. Start with broad, quantitative data. In this case, pull a comprehensive report on all widget sales for the last several quarters or years.

Understand. Next, leverage your team. In roundtables or one-on-ones, talk to people with relevant knowledge and experience. In this case, bring together the member of your leadership team responsible for the widget product design, the one in charge of quality assurance, and the documentation lead. What's going on with the red widgets? Did we expect feedback like this? What might be done to address it?

Assess. Once you have enough context, go directly to those involved. In this case, you or your team might contact the customer support representatives who have been fielding complaints about red widgets. Do the people who buy red widgets instead of green widgets share demographic factors? Are there compounding factors that adversely affect these clients in particular? What about people who don't have problems installing red widgets—what do they have in common?

Support. Once you've fully explored the problem and its possible root causes, you may already have a course of action in mind. Regardless of how you proceed, confirm with the original hand raiser that you have heard and *understood* the problem as they see it. If workers don't see support for their concerns, they won't bother raising their hands the next time they see a problem.

Hypothesize. Doing nothing is underrated. In many cases, employees exaggerate problems. Not deliberately, but because they have a narrower view of the picture. A disproportionate response to a relatively minor issue can cause more trouble than it resolves. Sometimes, a clear picture emerges only after more time passes and more data is gathered. As you learn to be less reactive as a leader, you discover that many seemingly urgent issues resolve themselves.

On the other hand, if your investigation reveals a clear path forward, take a measured approach with a small experiment. See if the results match your hypothesis. If so, go bigger and see whether the trend continues. If the results don't match up, think of a better explanation. Again, the idea here is to stay deliberate and strategic even as the alarm bells are ringing. The temptation will always be to overplay your hand. QUASH the problem instead to identify the underlying pattern.

Despite that knee-jerk reaction to shut down red widget production, the data (**Quantify**) shows that red widget sales are actually flat, while green widget sales have declined 17 percent over the last three quarters. Talking to your direct reports (**Understand**), you learn that the green widgets work more seamlessly because they've been refined over several years. The red widgets are new and need kinks worked out, but they have more long-term potential. Also, the customer service reps report that there were only a handful of complaints out of thousands sold (**Assess**), primarily by new customers who have never previously purchased any widgets.

After thanking the reps for running the problem up the flagpole (**Support**), you decide that waiting for the red widgets' kinks to resolve at this pace doesn't make sense. New customers buying new products like the red widgets represent the company's future. They're too valuable to leave in the dark while bugs and quirks are gradually worked out. Instead of diverting the company's attention to the older green widgets and shutting down production of the new, more promising red widgets to make the problem go away, you sunset the fading green widgets in certain markets (**Hypothesis**) and devote everyone's attention to refining the red widgets. This includes improving the installation documentation and creating an onboarding process for new customers so that they have a better idea of what to expect from the product.

Transitioning from problems to patterns is tricky for those new to authority because, until we're in charge, we're rewarded for solving problems quickly and efficiently. That makes us want to be *seen* as solving problems quickly and efficiently. This is a scaled-up version of the *performative* work trap we discussed in **BRUTAL**. Solving a problem directly instead of helping the team solve the pattern is performative work for leaders. You must multiply the impact you made as an individual contributor. That's why you have a team! Once again, a behavior that served us well in one stage of our careers has become a disadvantage in another.

Problems are fun because they have a beginning, middle, and end. You notice them, work on them, and solve them. Patterns are complex and open-ended. It takes skill and experience to separate the signal from the noise, and it takes leadership to prioritize addressing them over the urgent, more easily fixable problems that emerge regularly.

FAIL-SAFE FEEDBACK

As we've seen, being **BOSSY** involves more *understanding* and *helping* than *deciding* and *ordering*. One of the most important forms of help you can offer is feedback. You'll discover that top performers *crave* feedback.

If you have a talented team that operates at a high level, chances are they possess a robust growth mindset. On the other hand, for those less skilled or motivated, you owe it to them to share how they can level up. Performance doesn't improve through osmosis. Where top performers crave feedback, bottom performers *need* it.

In other words, take your hands off the wheel, but don't kick your feet up. Leadership is an action, not a position. We *all* have areas of improvement, and no one is better placed to identify and address those areas than the team's leader. When you spot a rough edge, give that employee the information they need to sand it down.

Just don't overdo it. In my first few years as a manager, I gave feedback on nearly everything my direct reports did. If you showed me a twenty-slide deck, you'd get at least three or four comments a slide. This was my insecurity rearing its head. I wanted to show them I was invested, but I overwhelmed them instead. I learned to focus on a handful of macro issues and ignore the micro stuff. Otherwise, you stop adding value and start draining morale.

(You can find feedback scripts for a direct report, colleague, or partner at **wildcouragebook.com/resources**.)

Another morale-killing habit among managers is staying silent until something goes wrong. Even a minor point of criticism lands hard when it's the only feedback an employee receives for weeks. There's a huge asymmetry in how human beings process information. Because of this negativity bias, "the propensity to attend to, learn from, and use negative information far more than positive information," we must deliver copious amounts of positive feedback to balance the scales. Effective managers deliver a steady drip of encouragement so that course corrections don't erode trust and goodwill. We can all take tough love occasionally if it's leavened with plenty of regular love.

Remember, aim for a five-to-one ratio: five positives for every negative. The positives can be anything: a high five here, a "great job on that report" there. Even the occasional happy-face emoji. A single negative comment can be crushing unless it's cushioned by enough positive ones.

———

Giving constructive feedback can be a minefield, depending on the organization's culture and the vibe you've established with your team. The best way to navigate those mines is to rely on a consistent system everyone on the team understands. Otherwise, your feedback may strike some as capricious or arbitrary.

Next time, stay SAFE:

Setting. Instead of offering feedback in general, address a recent instance of the problematic behavior and say when and where it happened: "Let's talk about your presentation at last week's partner meeting." Be specific even if the behavior happens frequently.

Action. Describe the behavior in simple and concrete terms without editorializing or catastrophizing what happened: "You talked over senior leaders three times."

Feeling. Once you've identified the problem, seek to understand the other person's intention before going further: "What were you feeling when this was happening?" This gives them a chance to say, "Oh, wow. My intention was not at all to talk over them. I was anxious that we wouldn't get to the end of the presentation, which covered the data the senior leaders had specifically requested."

Effect. Acknowledge their intention yet explain the negative outcome of the behavior: "Ah, that makes sense. You were nervous about not getting to the analysis; however, cutting people off this way made you seem impatient and less collaborative than I know you are."

From there, brainstorm simple ways to improve. For example, someone with the bad habit of talking over others—including yours truly—might count to three after anyone else stops talking before continuing. It's a solvable problem.

Specificity and objectivity are crucial. We all learn differently, and many of us struggle to absorb or act on abstract feedback. For example, telling someone they "always" talk over others may frustrate or confuse them. After all, every conversation has an ebb and flow, and it's natural to experience some overlap. By drilling down to a specific instance, you cut past what happened and focus on the disconnect between the person's intentions and the real-world outcome.

You can also instill in your team a practice of **one up, one opp**. Whenever someone presents or delivers a project, you share one thing they did well (up) and one opportunity for improvement (opp). This builds the muscle of giving feedback (which many managers don't), keeps it light, and avoids overwhelm. It's a forcing function for giving feedback immediately instead of waiting for the next performance review. For example, when walking to the parking lot after a client presentation:

- Your one up is that you used more hard data in your slides this time—it was compelling.

- Your one opp is that you should avoid "you know" as filler language to continue rocking these presentations.

SAFE feedback gives the other person everything they need to improve. You're telling them exactly what they did and why that wasn't the right approach. And if they have several material areas of development and don't improve after being given ample chances, be **BRUTAL** and let them go. Don't sit on it. You know where this is going.

This section focuses on constructive coaching, but positive coaching for a top performer is critical, too. This should go beyond coaching on their day-to-day. You could coach and support them toward their next, higher-profile role. Remember, good talent is rented, not owned.

TRAIT TRAPS

Don't break people

"People who worked on *30 Rock* all moved away as fast as they could when it was over," Tina Fey, reflecting on her leadership as an executive producer, told Conan O'Brien on his podcast, "because I think we broke them. I think we broke a lot of people. It was a loving staff, and there was a lot of pride, and we did a lot of good work, but I think a lot of people never want to see us again."

In **OBSESSED**, I pointed to Tina Fey's extraordinary work ethic as a writer for *Saturday Night Live*. For example, she started work on each weekly episode a full day earlier than her peers. This approach served Fey as an individual contributor but made her a challenging boss.

If we're **OBSESSED**, we expect those on our team to be as committed and hardworking as we were in their position. Before you decide they're falling short of your bar, remember that, as an individual contributor, you saw your work ethic firsthand. Your boss wasn't there when you stayed late preparing that presentation. Or deliberated over that email pitch for far longer than strictly necessary. Only you knew how much of your exercise, shower, or commute time was spent dreaming up product features or planning a more efficient schedule for the day.

Your work ethic is always transparent to you. The efforts of your direct reports are often opaque. If you expect the people on your team to *look* as busy and hardworking on the outside as *you feel* on the inside, you will be disappointed and frustrated. Then these miscalibrated expectations will come out in the form of unrealistic quotas, hallucinatory milestones, or a wildly unbalanced feedback–praise ratio.

Don't break people. Treating colleagues this way is not only unfair and unethical but also counterproductive. People function at their best when they feel appreciated and valued for their efforts. Hold people accountable, but always give them the benefit of the doubt. Remember that you're seeing only a fraction of their effort. Adjust your expectations accordingly.

Don't be toxic

The word *toxic* gets thrown around liberally. If you want to be a better manager, it helps to ground your understanding of toxic leadership in real-life behaviors. These represent some of the more common variations:

Ridicule and personal criticism. Never be condescending or otherwise demean the people who work under you. Early in my career, when I was in a strategy and operations role, my manager asked with a half laugh, "Do you know how models work?" I was one of the only people on the team without a McKinsey background, and I did feel like I was in over my head. Didn't matter. As a manager, he should have taken the time to coach me on model building or guided me to a mentor. He was incredibly smart but a miserable manager.

Similarly, never offer feedback about someone's personality. Instead of "you need to be less shy in meetings," try, "You will have an even greater impact on this project if you amplify your voice in meetings." Instead of "you need to be less aggressive," try, "The project will be successful if you learn each stakeholder's communication style and collaborate with them based on that."

As the saying goes, it's not what you did or said but how you made someone feel. It's rarely the project, analysis, or model that makes people lose sleep at night, causes anxiety, or leads to attrition. It's the behaviors that do. When you're a manager, the effects of your bad behaviors are amplified. Use your power responsibly.

Urgency and anger. By default, make most things you ask of your team a minimum five-business-day turnaround. Unless you're running a hospital, you're not saving lives. It's your job to plan ahead instead of running things with a constant degree of urgency. Give people ample time to prepare, and reserve the fire drills for when you smell something burning.

Likewise, never use bold text, all caps, exclamation points, or any other form of emphasis in communicating with your team unless it's positive. There is an imbalance of power. When you are a manager, every whisper is a shout. Everything you do, positive and negative, lands harder. This stuff is the email equivalent of red-faced screaming—which is also, for the record, worth avoiding.

Envy and credit stealing. As discussed, there is no need to worry about credit where your team is involved. When they win, you win. Hire people smarter than you, help them succeed, and then get out of their way. Let them know that not only can they be better than you, *your job is to coach them to be better than they think they can be.* That's the real magic.

You'll find that the only thing more valuable to an organization than being a top performer is being someone who can hire, lead, and, most important, *retain* top performers.

Inconsistency and unpredictability. Teams thrive in a stable environment. Your job is to create that environment and to protect your team from all the chaos outside that environment. Say what you mean, mean what you say, and stay on track—in short, be **BRUTAL**.

You can never be sure what a toxic manager will say or do next. It creates an enormous amount of tension for the team. As my dad likes to say, even if you're on an even keel, shit flows downhill in an organization. When a VP goes into a tailspin about a problem, that puts the director in a tailspin, which puts the manager in a tailspin. No one can do their best work in that kind of environment.

Build a dam and stop the chaos. Shield your team from any indecision and inconsistency raining down from above. That lets them focus on their work instead of the drama.

Indecisiveness. The team looks to you for guidance. Don't waste forty-five minutes of an hour-long meeting trying to collectively arrive at the right coverage plan for Troy's paternity leave. (I've done things like this, and in each case, my team very much wished I hadn't.) Listening and collaboration matter, but you must decide. If your title is "director," direct. Don't hem and haw, don't try to please everyone on small decisions, and don't go back and forth once you have decided. Be **BRUTAL** about what is most important.

Playing favorites. Look at each direct report's unique strengths, and play to those strengths. Focus 75 percent of your energy as a manager on an employee's strengths and the rest on development areas. This means you must *see* them for their strengths. Everyone has them. Be mindful of the bias to value those who share the same strengths, backgrounds, and style as you.

To be clear, I believe that most of the time these toxic actions are not malicious but the result of ignorance, lack of self-awareness, and lack of proper management training, or, frankly, most often, leaders moving too fast. Making a close study of these behaviors is a great way to start noticing areas of improvement in your own management style.

You may not lead a team. If you're a solo entrepreneur or freelancer, you may have no interest in ever doing so. It doesn't matter. **BOSSY** is as important as much as any other **Trait**. As a freelancer, you often have to get **BOSSY** with a client. That's because regardless of your profession or pursuit, being **BOSSY** is about recruiting support, leveraging talent and expertise, offering constructive feedback, keeping projects on track, making decisions based on the data, and much more. Ignore this **Trait** at your peril.

To lead, you need it all: curiosity, obsession, the willingness to influence others. . . . You must create so much benefit for others that people are drawn to join you in your quest.

Find and cultivate allies, partners, and collaborators. Help them aggressively. Push them constantly. Michael Jordan relentlessly needled his teammates to do better. He wouldn't let them underperform. Challenging as it was to play with him, they were grateful—he made them champions.

BOSSY
Steer others to success

- **Hands off the wheel.** As a leader, you get more credit for helping others do their jobs than for doing it yourself. Step back and give your team what they need to grow. Fifty percent of your job is managing up, down, and across.

- **Be a set rat.** Take it slow in any new leadership role. Shadow until you understand the problems you hope to solve. Aim to observe someone on your team for one hour a week—not to criticize, but to empathize.

- **Patterns, not problems.** As a leader, you must not miss the forest for the trees. Lead with an iterative, data-driven, holistic approach to your team's biggest challenges. QUASH the temptation to have a knee-jerk reaction (quantify, understand, assess, support, and hypothesize).

- **Fail-safe feedback.** Maintain morale and improve performance with early, clear, and constructive feedback and highlight each SAFE element: setting, action, feeling, effect. Never assume your team knows what they're doing well or what they could improve.

- **Don't break people.** Push your team to excel, but be mindful of their well-being and give them the benefit of the doubt. Don't expect them to look as busy on the outside as you felt on the inside when you were in their shoes.

- **Don't be toxic.** Don't let the pressure of leadership turn you into a monster. Contempt, anger, and jealous behavior have no place in the workplace.

Conclusion

Embrace a life of wild courage

Though I've emphasized hands-on tactics in each chapter, the nine Traits underpin them all. Let's review these nine powerful words one more time:

- **WEIRD:** The courage to stand out.

- **SELFISH:** The courage to stand up for what you want.

- **SHAMELESS:** The courage to stand behind your efforts and abilities.

- **OBSESSED:** The courage to set your own standard.

- **NOSY:** The courage to dig deeper.

- **MANIPULATIVE:** The courage to influence others.

- **BRUTAL:** The courage to protect your time and energy.

- **RECKLESS:** The courage to take calculated risks.

- **BOSSY:** The courage to listen and lead.

It's no accident the word *courage* appears in every definition and throughout each chapter of the book. We focus so much on merit and skill in our society that we miss the obvious fact that lasting success goes to those who try, try, and try again.

Some of the most brilliant and talented people in history fell short of their potential because they weren't able to deal with the fear involved in pursuing worthwhile goals:

- Fear of the unknown,

- fear of discomfort,

- fear of failure, and

- most of all, *fear of the judgment of others.*

Muster the wild courage to chase what you want in life, and you'll discover a vital truth: whether you succeed or fail at doing any one thing, you'll never feel as purposeful, powerful, and alive as when you're pushing through fear toward the wonder and joy on the other side. As I said at the beginning of this book, everything you've ever wanted is waiting for you on the other side of fear. It's right there waiting for you—**reach for it.**

This book is my earnest attempt to help you achieve *all* your cherished goals, the personal and professional objectives that, secretly or not, occupy a large part of your heart and mind. Using these nine powerful, wild words, I've sought to help you and even push you to adopt a new, empowered mindset. If you're willing to embrace these **Traits** and the behaviors they describe, I believe you can achieve absolutely anything.

With wild courage, a life of boundless adventure and possibility awaits.

I'm rooting for you. Let's go.

TO PARTNER FURTHER

We help organizations and individuals cultivate Wild Courage in many ways. To help accelerate your career or support your team in becoming more effective, we offer:

- Custom **keynotes** and **fireside chats** that align with your team's current challenges and needs.

- Interactive **workshops and trainings** based on goals you identify to make the learnings in the book extra sticky.

- **Licensing IP** so your entire organization or company can benefit from how this book helps you pursue your goals and achieve them.

- **One-on-one coaching** based on the Wild Courage frameworks to help you achieve your most ambitious goals.

Most services are available both in person and virtually.

Shoot us an email at book@itsjennywood.com to discuss how we can help you. (By getting in touch, you are putting three traits into practice: **NOSY**, **MANIPULATIVE**, and **BOSSY**. Well done.)

Let's do this,

Jenny Wood

P.S.: You also might enjoy my free newsletter that's full of bite-sized, actionable tips for success. You can sign up at wildcouragebook.com/newsletter.
And, of course, feel free to email simply to let me know what you thought of the book! hello@itsjennywood.com

HELP OTHERS DISCOVER
THEIR OWN WILD COURAGE

If you gained value from this book, I'd be honored if you wrote a review on Amazon, Google, or Goodreads.

Instructions are at **wildcouragebook.com/resources**.

Me asking you to do this? Completely **SHAMELESS**!

Acknowledgments

David Moldawer, you are extraordinarily talented, and I'm grateful you agreed to put that talent into *Wild Courage*. You gave me a genius homework assignment on my flight back from New York. Then, this book was born.

Lisa DiMona, there's a reason bestselling authors unite in the proclamation, "In Lisa we trust." You made this project so much fun with your no-nonsense kindness, skill, and insight. Thank you Chaim Lipskar, Peggy Boulos Smith, Kate Boggs, Maja Nikolic, and everyone on the Writers House team for selling this book worldwide.

Lydia Yadi, everyone who's worked with you said I'd be lucky to land you as an editor. What an understatement. You brought such value, craft, dedication, and humor to this project. Thank you also to Adrian Zackheim, Niki Papadopoulos, Margot Stamas, Stephanie Bowen, Rachael Perriello Henry, Zehra Kayi, Heather Faulls, Kirstin Berndt, Megan McCormack, and everyone on the Penguin Random House and Portfolio teams.

Mike Harpley. You rallied a magnificent army to support *Wild Courage* at Pan Macmillan. Thank you for your trust and partnership and to

Josie Turner, Jamie Forrest, Leanne Williams, and the entire team for believing in me and this book.

Barbara Cave Henricks, Pam Peterson Coviello, and everyone at CHC, thank you for being PR ninjas and crafting the message of *Wild Courage* so beautifully.

Thank you to those who shared their stories for this project and hundreds more who offered: Annabella Losco, Bharati Nayudu, Greg Fatticci, Karthick Sivanadian, Nick Ricucci, and Tracy Moore.

Pre-readers, thank you for the helpful insight, pushback, and tweaks.

Wild Courage Launch Team: thank you for your enthusiasm, which helped get this book to its first several thousand readers.

Eric Tobias, thank you for helping me see around corners. You've been a critical confidant, adviser, and friend. And thank you, Amy Hartman and Emily Cooper, for being best-in-class.

Thank you to Kimberly Harrington for the wild idea. You were a blast to work with.

Lauren Kinney. You are a gifted writer, and you gave me the gift of a second chance. I'm so grateful. And thank you to Kelley Hill.

Courtney Kenney. Thank you for sharing a slice of your knowledge and expertise, which is vast.

Tracey Madigan, your emotional-mapping strategy is a game changer.

Tim Grahl, thank you for your generosity and killer insights—even if you got roped into this by Chad Cannon. Chad Cannon, thank you for roping in the best people and being so great yourself.

To the tens of thousands of Own Your Career participants, thank you for giving me the opportunity to partner in your career at Google. Marta Caetani, OYC simply would not exist without your incredible abilities. You are a special talent. Ali Gardner, thank you for the endless dedication, ideas, and heart you poured into the program. You both will go far. Thanks also to the OYC volunteer core team: Ariel Hathaway, Elena Solomon Thorpe, Eliza Epstein, and Uzo Biosah.

To Mike Miller for your unparalleled leadership and to so many other leaders who inspire me: Ted Buell, Sam Sebastian, Anas Osman, Anwar Akram, Debbie Weinstein, Erica Fox, Estee Cheng, John Black, Kate Stanford, Maggie Hulce, Michelle Bandler, Arijit Sarker, Scott Falzone, Tim Moynihan, and Vanessa Hartley.

Thank you to those who go above and beyond to support passion projects at work: Aarthi Scott, Alan Moss, Allan Thygesen, April Anderson, Bethany Sitto, Bhavna Chhabra, Brian Glaser, Charles Scrase, David Sneddon, Elise Birkhofer, Emmanuel Sauquet, Imma Calvo, Jennifer Petoff, Jenny Dairyko, Julie Krueger, Kate Kohlbrenner, Kate Stanford, Kellie Fitzgerald, Kyle Keogh, Laura Orland, Lauren McLane, Leah Smart, Lowell Doppelt, Madhuri Duggirala, Mary Ellen Coe, Mary Hamershock, Matt Brittin, Melody Olson, Philipp Schindler, Rebecca Wahl, Rob McClung, and Tara Walpert Levy.

To some of the brightest authors in the space. Seth Godin, you pushed me to think deeply about how I want to spend my remaining cycles around the sun. Kim Scott, you're a rare find as a leader and mentor. Thank you for believing in this project from day one. Dan Pink, you taught me to, "Write the book I want to write and stand behind it 100 percent." Smart advice. Gretchen Rubin, thank you for telling me that I already had the answers. Cal Newport, thanks for teaching me to work poetically. Adam Grant, thanks for all the launch insights. Alan Eagle: Thanks for suggesting that I define each trait in my own words. Mo Bunnell, thank you for giving so much of yourself to help me grow. Tiago Forte, thank you for creating the room. Ali Abdaal and Izzy Sealey: thank you for your generosity and the Uber brain dump. Anne-Laure Le Cunff, thank you for being my sister-in-books. Noah Kagan: thanks for juggling Mafc in labor and texting me launch tips—on Shabbos no less. And thank you to Billy Broas, Dafna Michaelson Jenet, Dorie Clark, Eric Partaker, Jim Kwik, Jim Lecinski, Khe Hy, Liz Fosslien, Melody Wilding, Michael Bungay Stanier, Mike Michalowicz, Mollie West Duffy, Nir Eyal, Paul Kix, Russ Laraway, Sahil Bloom, Tara Mohr, and Vanessa Van Edwards.

Thank you to so many advisers in the author, creator, and entrepreneur space: Alisa Cohn, Amanda Goetz, Amanda Northcutt, Angelina Krahn, Brennan Dunn, Brittany Hodak, Charlie Hoehn, Chris Lee, Dan Shipper, Darrell Vesterfelt, Emily Lavelle, Gretchen Leslie, Hannah Gross, Ines Lee, Jenna Buffaloe, Jo Franco, Joe Hudson, Jonny and Kelly Miller, Josh Kaufman, Justin Welsh, Kathryn Valentine, Kelley Hill, Kevin Espiritu, Kim Kaupe, Kim Rittberg, Laura Gassner Otting, Lorraine Lee, Meighan Cavanaugh, Michael Brown, Mike Pacchione, Mike Rucker, Nathan Barry, Nausheen Chen, Nick Lewis, Nick Milo, Nicolas Cole, Patrice Poltzer, Paul Carr, Paul Millerd, Rosalind Wiseman, Ryder Carroll, Sarah Lacy, Shawn Blanc, Stephen Hutson, Tara Mosier, Terry Rice, Tim Gillies, and Wes Kao.

To teammates, friends, and family who helped shape these ideas over the last two decades: Allison Lehmann, Allison Schwartz, Amy Mahoney, Annabel Botterill, Ari Yeskel, Arik Orbach, Bianca Livi, Brianne Reeber, Carol and Jay Scheiner, Carrie Garcia, David Moerlein, Deepa Reddy, Emily DuBois, Fred Faber, Greg Perlstein, Harry Griffin, Jackie Rogowski, Jane Bernier, Jeff Jaworski, Jen Miller, Jo Schaalman, John Krebsbach, Judy Illes, Karen Carlucci Freni, Kate Sochacki Kathleen Kempe, Kimberly Frost, Kimberly Neckers, Lauren Epshteyn, Lauren Hernstein, Lauren Statman, Liz Barnum, Lori and Michael Koffler, Meghna Greenwald, Melissa Porter, Meredith Clark, Mollie Williams, Nancy Hwang, Natalie Wasielewski, Neil Hoyne, Nina Temple, Nitesh Misra, Patty Devlin, Paul Holman-Kursky, Phillip Park, Rachel Burke, Rachel Meyers, Ryan Perry, Sam Grigsby, Sheri Gurock, and Ting Zhang.

Aarushi Dedhiya, thank you for the dedicated book research and for your heroic efforts in keeping us up-to-date on social media. Rocci Alvarez, you jumped right in with precision, speed, and thoughtfulness. Thank you also to all the interns who helped with the launch.

Laura Mae Martin, it's been an honor to follow in your footsteps in so many ways. Your success and kindness have always inspired me.

Martin Gonzalez, you made this project so much fun. Thank you for the book-launch nuggets and second-mover advantages you gave me.

Lexi Reese, there are two kinds of people in life: those who open up their Rolodex to you and those who don't. Thanks for being the former.

Christina Wire, your wisdom helped me live the values of my own book when I was scared. You are a gem of a leader and friend.

Jonathan Fields, thank you for your wisdom on our strategy hikes. You're another rare-find Rolodex-opener and a wonderful human.

Kelly Schaefer, thank you for telling me what kind of stock you would buy. Your sharp insight and thoughtfulness were critical to my sanity over the past few years.

Thank you, Donna Stapleton. You've been a gift to this project with kindness and quick wit.

Thank you, Jenny Blake, for helping me find this new path and being a trusted confidant throughout the ups and downs of this adventure. You are an inspiration to me.

Jason Feifer, I would not be here without you. Thank you for the vision you had for this project on your parents' back porch and for every voice memo since then.

Thank you, Faith Brozovich, for helping me drop the rope with the anxiety monster and helping me realize I needed to move along the spectrum from security to enhancement. Also, thank you to Lisa Kentgen and Bennett Leslie; you are both so talented at what you do.

Julie Connolly, you are a gift to anyone you work with. Thank you for helping me see that my circumstances had changed. Zach Hawkins, thank you for shaping my thinking paths.

Lois Smith Brady, the way you captured our subway story and shared it with the world created a flywheel of serendipity. Thank you for this gift.

Carlina Villalpando Daugherty, when you told me you reinstated band practice on a closed-off field by calling the superintendent at home, it was obvious you were the perfect partner on this book launch. This project could not have happened without you. Thank you for your strategic mindset, organization, and, truly, for everything.

Randi Larson and Marcia Segall, *Wild Courage* was born somewhere along North Shanahan Fork with you. Every touchpoint matters, and each one with you two makes me happy. Thank you for being so smart, funny, and real.

Stefanie Mirman, please join me in visualizing this written in the sky, "Stef: You are amazing. Thank you for the unwavering friendship since 1982."

To Duain Wolfe, Deborah DeSantis, Mary Louise Burke, and the entire past and present staff of the Colorado Children's Chorale, thank you for helping thousands of children discover their courage and excellence. Mr. Wolfe, you made me stand every rehearsal for misbehaving. Smart move. The rigor you taught me translated to all the positive lessons I teach in this book.

Thank you, Maria Godoy Saenz, for being our CEO with so much love, kindness, and patience.

To all my siblings, thank you for your love and support: Karli Illes, Rachel Rosenberg-Shoch, Daniel Shoch, Dan Rosenberg, Becca Rosenberg, Jonathan Rosenberg, Teresa Rosenberg, Jaime Brody, Meghan Todd, Jeremy Brody, and Anna Graves.

To Susan and Bill Wood: thank you for being such a wonderful Bubbie and Grandpa, for the musical and memorable seders, and for cheering this project along.

Audrey Halpern and Steven Rosenberg, thank you for being so kind and generous, being such an outstanding Mimi and Pa, and rolling with all my "salmon" chases.

Ricki Illes, you are on every page of *Wild Courage*. Thank you for the lessons in empathy, strategy, and relationship-building. And thanks for continuing to remind me, at forty-five, to look both ways before I leap into the street. You could write the book on how to ace it as a mom.

Leslie Illes, this project is a big l'dor v'dor of every business, influence, and life lesson you taught me. Thank you for trusting me with your stories in this book and for always helping me prioritize what is most important in life: family.

Ari and Noa, thank you for your grace while I wrote and for understanding the trade-offs it required. You are wild and courageous in all the best ways. Ari, your energy, tenacity, and kindness will take you far. Noa, your empathy, pizzazz, and strength will take you far.

Jon, when I chased that stranger off the subway, I hoped he'd be self-assured, empathetic, smart, and sarcastic. You were all these things. And then you also made me laugh out loud. Thank you for your patience, wisdom, and edits as I tackled this book. When I told you I wanted to embark on this crazy adventure, I warned you I might not be able to do dishes for a few years. You responded, "You've got this, babe. I've got the dishes." And you did. I love you.

Thank you to the Metropolitan Transportation Authority. You draw a great crowd.

And finally, to you. You could have chosen to spend the past several hours anywhere and you chose to spend it here. Thank you for giving me an opportunity to contribute to your goals.

Notes

EPIGRAPH

ix **I believe it may:** Eileen Levy, "Poet Says Her Love of Poetry Grew Despite Poverty," *Lexington (KY) Herald*, April 12, 1979, A3.

GATHER YOUR COURAGE

12 **"certain human brain areas":** Jaak Panksepp, "Feeling the Pain of Social Loss," *Science* 302, no. 5643 (October 10, 2003): 237–39, doi.org/10.1126/science.1091062.

13 **"Stefani Germanotta, you will never":** Lauren Bohn, "When They Dissed the Future Lady Gaga," *The World*, January 17, 2016, theworld.org/stories/2016-01-17/when-they-dissed-future-lady-gaga.

CHAPTER 1. **WEIRD: WIN AS YOU OR LOSE AS "WHO?"**

17 **(adj.): of strange or extraordinary:** *Merriam-Webster*, s.v. "weird (*adj.*)," accessed August 28, 2023, merriam-webster.com/dictionary/weird.

19 **After World War II ended:** Roman Mars, "On Average," August 23, 2016, in *99% Invisible*, produced by Avery Trufelman, podcast, MP3 audio, 21:36, 99percentinvisible.org/episode/on-average.

21 **Jason Feifer, editor in chief:** Silvia Bellezza, Francesca Gino, and Anat Keinan, "The Red Sneakers Effect: Inferring Status and Competence from Signals of Nonconformity," *Journal of Consumer Research* 41, no. 1 (June 2014): 35–54, doi.org/10.1086/674870.

22 **"work outcomes such as job":** Ralph van den Bosch and Toon W. Taris, "Authenticity at Work: Development and Validation of an Individual Authenticity Measure at Work," *Journal of Happiness Studies* 15, no. 1 (February 2014): 1–18, doi.org/10.1007/s10902-013-9413-3.

32 **When the NBA fined:** KicksOnFirecom, "Banned Air Jordan 1 Commercial," posted February 25, 2010, YouTube, video, https://www.youtube.com/watch?v=eEmAgKYVluo.

CHAPTER 2. SELFISH: BE YOUR OWN CHAMPION

37 **(adj.): concerned excessively:** *Merriam-Webster*, s.v. "selfish (*adj.*)," accessed August 28, 2023, https://www.merriam-webster.com/dictionary/selfish.

40 **Brain scans show:** Lane Beckes, James A. Coan, and Karen Hasselmo, "Familiarity Promotes the Blurring of Self and Other in the Neural Representation of Threat," *Social Cognitive and Affective Neuroscience* 8, no. 6 (August 2013): 670–77, doi.org /10.1093/scan/nss046.

48 **Likewise, the band:** Craig Jenkins, "Clare Torry's Voice Is Seared into Your Brain Whether You Know It or Not," *Vulture*, January 10, 2020, vulture.com/2020/01/clare -torry-pink-floyd-dark-side-of-the-moon.html.

54 **Economists describe the "second-mover":** "The Second-Mover Advantage," *Kellogg Insight*, November 4, 2013, insight.kellogg.northwestern.edu/article/the_second_move r_advantage.

55 **Unlike the overly cooperative:** Veronique Greenwood, "These Ants Explode, but Their Nests Live to See Another Day," *New York Times*, April 23, 2018, nytimes.com /2018/04/23/science/exploding-ants.html.

CHAPTER 3. SHAMELESS: FIND YOUR SWAGGER

57 **(adj.): insensible to disgrace:** *Merriam-Webster*, s.v. "shameless (*adj.*)," accessed August 28, 2023, https://www.merriam-webster.com/dictionary/shameless.

74 **If Harry Styles enjoys:** "Harry Styles Talks Quarantine, Fine Line & 1D's 10 Year Anniversary," *Zach Sang Show*, April 3, 2020, YouTube video, 12:59, youtube.com /watch?v=Uq9cEOM8VOM.

76 **This is the assumption:** Dale T. Miller and Cathy McFarland, "Pluralistic Ignorance: When Similarity Is Interpreted as Dissimilarity," *Journal of Personality and Social Psychology* 53, no. 2 (August 1987): 298–305, doi.org/10.1037/0022-3514.53.2.298.

CHAPTER 4. OBSESSED: PUSH, PERFORM, AND PERSIST

83 **(adj.): preoccupied with or haunted:** *Merriam-Webster*, s.v. "obsessed," accessed August 22, 2023, merriam-webster.com/dictionary/obsessed.

86 **Why make the application process easier:** Minda Zetlin, "Google Automatically Rejects Most Resumes for Common Mistakes You've Probably Made Too," *Inc.*, April 9, 2018, inc.com/minda-zetlin/google-resume-mistakes-laszlo-bock-job-hiring-employment .html.

86 **A behavioral study conducted:** Ellen Langer, Arthur Blank, and Benzion Chanowitz, "The Mindlessness of Ostensibly Thoughtful Action: The Role of 'Placebic' Information in Interpersonal Interaction," *Journal of Personality and Social Psychology* 36, no. 6 (June 1978): 635–42, doi.org/10.1037/0022-3514.36.6.635.

91 **Craftsmanship, according to Crawford:** Matthew B. Crawford, *Shop Class as Soulcraft: An Inquiry into the Value of Work* (New York: Penguin Books, 2010).

99 **In 2011, professors Michael I. Norton:** Michael I. Norton, Daniel Mochon, and Dan Ariely, "The 'IKEA Effect': When Labor Leads to Love" (Harvard Business School Working Paper 11-091, 2011), available at https://www.hbs.edu/ris/Publication%20Files /norton%20mochon%20ariely_6f7b1134-06ef-4940-a2a5-ba1b3be7e47e.pdf.

100 **when you have only six:** Conan O'Brien, "Tina Fey," October 13, 2019, in *Conan O'Brien Needs a Friend*, produced by Matt Gourley, podcast, MP3 audio, 50:58, teamcoco.com /podcasts/conan-obrien-needs-a-friend/episodes/tina-fey.

105 **Psychologist Barry Schwartz:** Barry Schwartz, *The Paradox of Choice: Why More Is Less*, rev. ed. (New York: HarperCollins e-books, 2009), 78.

CHAPTER 5. **NOSY:** GET INSATIABLY CURIOUS

111 **(adj.): of prying or inquisitive disposition:** *Merriam-Webster*, s.v. "nosy," accessed August 24, 2023, merriam-webster.com/dictionary/nosy.

114 **Children under five:** Michelle M. Chouinard, P. L. Harris, and Michael P. Maratsos, "Children's Questions: A Mechanism for Cognitive Development," *Monographs of the Society for Research in Child Development* 72, no. 1 (2007): 1–129.

114 **Researchers at UC Davis:** Matthias J. Gruber, Bernard D. Gelman, and Charan Ranganath, "States of Curiosity Modulate Hippocampus-Dependent Learning via the Dopaminergic Circuit," *Neuron* 84, no. 2 (October 22, 2014): 486–96, doi.org/10.1016 /j.neuron.2014.08.060.

121 **Research confirms Rachel's:** Diana I. Tamir and Jason P. Mitchell, "Disclosing Information about the Self Is Intrinsically Rewarding," *Proceedings of the National Academy of Sciences of the United States of America* 109, no. 21 (May 22, 2012): 8038–43, doi.org /10.1073/pnas.1202129109.

CHAPTER 6. **MANIPULATIVE:** BUILD INFLUENCE THROUGH EMPATHY

131 **(adj.): intended to control:** *Merriam-Webster*, s.v. "manipulate," accessed February 7, 2024, merriam-webster.com/dictionary/manipulate.

138 **"feeling excluded from":** King's College London, "Office Politics Can Be a Force for Good, New Research Shows," Phys.org, May 30, 2022, phys.org/news/2022-05-office -politics-good.html.

139 **"the ability of those":** Gerald R. Salancik and Jeffrey Pfeffer, "Who Gets Power—and How They Hold On to It," in *Readings in Managerial Psychology,* ed. Harold J. Leavitt, Louis R. Pondy, David M. Boje (Chicago: University of Chicago Press, 1989), 346.

140 **almost no disagreement:** Jeffrey Pfeffer, 7 *Rules of Power: Surprising—but True—Advice on How to Get Things Done and Advance Your Career* (Dallas, TX: Matt Holt, 2022).

153 **"If we hire a professional":** "Seth Godin: Authenticity Is Overrated. Here's What You Need Instead," Inc., July 31, 2020, YouTube video, 3:56, youtube.com/watch?v =lbJtuaFebtA.

CHAPTER 7. **BRUTAL:** DRAW LINES AND STICK TO THEM

159 **(adj.): unpleasantly accurate and incisive:** *Merriam-Webster*, s.v. "brutal," accessed February 7, 2024, merriam-webster.com/dictionary/brutal.

164 **According to fMRI research:** Juan F. Domínguez D, Sreyneth A. Taing, and Pascal Molenberghs, "Why Do Some Find It Hard to Disagree? An fMRI Study," *Frontiers in Human Neuroscience* 9 (January 2016): 718, doi.org/10.3389/fnhum.2015.00718.

171 **One analysis found:** Matt Plummer, "How to Spend Way Less Time on Email Every Day," *Harvard Business Review*, January 22, 2019, hbr.org/2019/01/how-to-spend-way-less-time-on-email-every-day.

171 **Bestselling author Neal Stephenson:** Neal Stephenson, "Why I Am a Bad Correspondent," *Neal Stephenson*, 2022, https://www.nealstephenson.com/why-i-am-a-bad-correspondent.html. .

CHAPTER 8. RECKLESS: ERR ON THE SIDE OF ACTION

183 **(adj.): marked by lack of proper caution:** *Merriam-Webster*, s.v. "reckless," accessed February 7, 2024, merriam-webster.com/dictionary/reckless.

186 **Research shows that you regret:** Adi Itzkin, Dina Van Dijk, and Ofer H. Azar, "At Least I Tried: The Relationship between Regulatory Focus and Regret Following Action vs. Inaction," *Frontiers in Psychology* 7 (October 2016): 1684, doi.org/10.3389/fpsyg.2016.01684.

187 **"Half of my blog posts":** Seth Godin, "Book Launch: The Practice," streamed live on November 3, 2020, Facebook video, 32:30, facebook.com/watch/live/?ref=watch_permalink&v=980847522407078.

189 **"What are you saving":** Jennifer Homans, "George Balanchine's Soviet Reckoning," *New Yorker*, September 5, 2022, newyorker.com/magazine/2022/09/12/george-balanchines-soviet-reckoning.

193 **"Time kills deals":** Terry Rice, "How to Write Proposals That Get Accepted and Don't Take Forever to Write," *Entrepreneur*, February 14, 2023, entrepreneur.com/starting-a-business/how-to-write-proposals-that-get-accepted-and-dont-take/444909.

CHAPTER 9. BOSSY: STEER OTHERS TO SUCCESS

201 **(adj.): inclined to domineer:** *Merriam-Webster*, s.v. "bossy," accessed July 18, 2024, merriam-webster.com/dictionary/bossy.

204 **Research shows that violating:** Gerben A. Van Kleef, Astrid C. Homan, Catrin Finkenauer, Seval Gündemir, and Eftychia Stamkou, "Breaking the Rules to Rise to Power: How Norm Violators Gain Power in the Eyes of Others," *Social Psychological and Personality Science* 2, no. 5 (September 2011): 500–507, doi.org/10.1177/1948550611398416.

213 **There's a huge asymmetry:** Amrisha Vaish, Tobias Grossmann, and Amanda Woodward, "Not All Emotions Are Created Equal: The Negativity Bias in Social-Emotional Development," *Psychological Bulletin* 134, no. 3 (May 2008): 383–403, doi.org/10.1037/0033-2909.134.3.383.

216 **"People who worked":** Conan O'Brien, "Tina Fey," October 13, 2019, in *Conan O'Brien Needs a Friend*, produced by Matt Gourley, podcast, MP3 audio, 50:58, teamcoco.com/podcasts/conan-obrien-needs-a-friend/episodes/tina-fey.